PLAY BALL Like the PROs

PLAY BALL Like the PROs

TIPS FOR KIDS FROM 20 BIG LEAGUE STARS

Steven Krasner

Ω

PEACHTREE

ATLANTA

For my father, Julius, who passed down to me
his passion for the game of baseball—
and for my son, Jeffrey, a better player than both of us,
who has carried on the family tradition

—*S. K.*

Ω

Published by
PEACHTREE PUBLISHERS, LTD.
1700 Chattahoochee Avenue
Atlanta, Georgia 30318-2112
www.peachtree-online.com

Text © 2002 Steven Krasner

Cover design by Loraine M. Balcsik
Interior design by Melanie M. McMahon

Manufactured in the United States of America

10 9 8 7 6 5 4 3 2

Library of Congress Cataloging-in-Publication Data

Krasner, Steven.
    Play ball like the pros : tips for kids from 20 big league stars /
written by Steven Krasner.-- 1st ed.
        p. cm.
    Summary: Nearly two dozen professional baseball players, such as Pedro
Martinez and Derek Jeter, provide insights into how they prepare for and
play the game.
    ISBN 1-56145-261-0
    1. Baseball for children--Juvenile literature. [1. Baseball. 2.
Baseball players.] I. Title.
    GV880.4 .K72 2002
    796.357'2--dc21
                                    2001007342

CONTENTS

★ ★

BATTER UP!

Game 1...

***The 2001 World Series, Arizona Diamondbacks versus the
New York Yankees...***

Arizona's Luis Gonzalez swings and connects squarely, sending the
baseball soaring up, up and away, over the fence at the Bank One
Ballpark in Phoenix.

It's a home run!

Obviously, that had to be a very special moment for Gonzalez, who
was 34 years old and playing in his first World Series game after 11
years in the big leagues.

But in a way, Gonzalez had lived this moment many times before.
As a kid, playing Wiffle ball in his backyard in Tampa, Florida,
Gonzalez would often pretend that he had just clouted a World Series
home run.

Now his dream had finally become a reality.

Probably every player who wears a big league uniform shares that
same childhood dream. And it's a pretty sure bet that the big leaguers
of the future are running around bases in a field somewhere right now,
dreaming similar dreams.

Of course, it takes more than just dreams to become a good baseball player. In this book, you'll find great tips from 20 big league stars
to help you improve your skills. The players will also share their own

childhood memories of playing ball, as well as the lessons they began learning at a very young age.

You may be surprised to find out that becoming a successful ballplayer isn't just about skills, or being born with superstar talent. It also has a lot to do with using your brain. Being smart on the baseball field—which includes the ability to make quick, accurate decisions—can help your team win. In each chapter of this book, there will be a tricky situation to test your baseball brain, as well as the best possible solution.

Sometimes, of course, things don't go well for even the smartest players. This can lead to some unusual—and occasionally embarrassing—moments that you'll also find recounted in this book. Baseballs have been known to bounce off an outfielder's head. Or roll into a beverage cup on the field. Or take bad hops at the very worst times.

But as they say around the big league diamonds, "That's baseball."

It's a great game. At any age.

Play ball!

PART 1

PITCHING

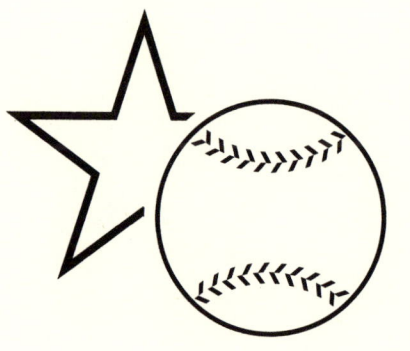

STRETCHING AND WARMING UP

Photograph courtesy of Seattle Mariners

AARON SELE

When a game begins, all eyes are on the pitcher. He starts his **windup,** his arm whips around, and he throws the ball to the plate. Even though that's the first pitch of the game, the act of throwing the ball didn't start just then for the pitcher. His preparation had begun much earlier that day.

In this chapter, All-Star Aaron Sele explains how to warm up properly before each game. He describes how and why a pitcher stretches and how he gets his arm loose before he even plays catch.

What's the first thing you should do to warm up when you get on the field?

First, you need to run. Pick two spots on your field, maybe from one **foul pole** to the other, and jog back and forth between them a couple of times. If your field doesn't have foul poles, then you can run from the right-field corner all the way to the left-field corner.

Second, you should run a few **sprints** to get your body warmed up and the blood flowing. That will help when you stretch, which is the next thing you should do.

What muscles do you need to stretch?

You should make sure you stretch your legs, your trunk, and then your arms. Make sure to stretch both your arms, even though you'll only throw with one. You need to get your whole body loose in order to get ready properly.

Why do you need to stretch? Why can't you just go out and throw?

When you stretch, your muscles become warm and loose. This will help to prevent injuries.

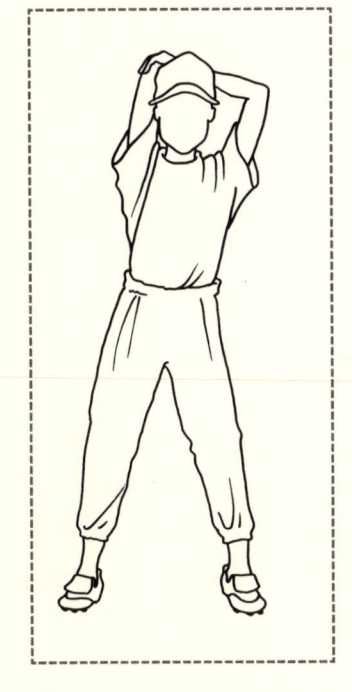

Why do you need to stretch your legs? You throw with your arm, right?

You need to stretch your legs because you generate your power from your legs.

You obviously throw the ball with your arm, but if you watch great pitchers such as Pedro Martinez, Roger Clemens, and Randy Johnson, you'll see they use the lower half of their bodies to push off the **rubber.** This helps them generate power in their pitching delivery. The power from their legs helps increase the power from their arms.

How do you stretch your arms?

There are some basic arm stretches you should do.

Place your elbow in the palm of your other hand. First, start with your right elbow in the palm of your left hand. Then pull that elbow slowly up and back over your head. Your elbow will point straight up past your right ear. That will stretch your arm.

After you've given your arm a good, steady stretch, pull your arm across your chest. To do this, hold the outside of your right elbow in the palm of your left hand and pull your elbow right across your chest. You want to hold your arm firm for about 10 seconds or so. If you feel as if your arm is tight, and you're having trouble getting it loose as you stretch, hold it across your chest a little longer and repeat the process a few times.

Repeat these exercises with your left arm.

After you're done stretching and you're ready to throw, should you pitch as hard as you can from your very first warm-up throw?

No. You don't want to start throwing too hard right away. There's a warming up process in the act of throwing. You should make sure to throw easily at first.

How far away should you be from the other person when you begin throwing?

You're not totally warmed up when you first start throwing. So you should keep a nice, short distance between you and the person with whom you're playing catch. That way, you can throw very lightly and easily and hit your partner in the chest. Any time you throw, you should always aim for the other person's chest. You want to make sure he's catching the ball right there with every throw.

Once your arm feels looser, and you start throwing the ball a little more firmly, you can back it up a bit. Put a little more distance between you and your partner. Remember, playing catch is not like pitching. You play catch just to loosen up. You're not going through your full pitching motion. There's no reason to throw all-out when you're warming up, especially from the beginning.

After playing catch for a while, then what do you do?

Once you're all stretched out and you've been throwing for a while so you're warmed up, it's time to head toward the mound. Throwing off the mound is different than throwing on flat ground, so you should throw to your catcher at half-speed first to get a feel of the mound. After you take maybe 5 to 7 throws, or whatever it takes to get your arm feeling loose from the mound, then you can start stretching it out and throwing harder.

Where do you aim to throw your pitches when you're warming up?

Your main goal is to throw strikes. If you have to throw the ball down the middle to throw strikes, then that's the most important thing. But whenever you practice pitching, you also want to practice "halves."

Halves are when you throw first to the outside half of the plate, and then to the inside half of the plate. You want to be able to throw the ball to both sides of the plate.

How do you grip the baseball?

There are a lot of different ways to hold the ball. But the best way to get a straight flight to home plate is by gripping the ball across the four **seams.** By that I mean holding the ball across the stitches, where they look like a horseshoe.

If you hold the ball this way, you'll get a **backspin** on the ball, with all four seams spinning when you release it. The four-seam fastball gives you the **truest flight.**

What happens if you hold the ball so that you have your fingers on the seams, instead of across them?

When you throw with your fingers on the seams, the ball has a tendency to **sink.** If you're a left-handed pitcher, the ball usually sinks to the left. If you're a right-handed pitcher, the ball will probably sink to the right. It's easier to control a four-seam fastball than a two-seam fastball, because the four-seamer tends to go straighter.

What's the position of your head as you throw a pitch?

I always say to aim your nose in the catcher's glove when you throw.

This will help you concentrate on getting your chest out over your knee as you move forward in your pitching delivery. If you do that, your head will be down toward your **target,** which will help you zero in on the target. It also causes you to release the ball out in front of you, as close to the catcher as possible.

What happens to your arm when you deliver a pitch?

Your arm will follow your head. If you pull your head to the left, your arm will go to the left. If you leave your head up, your arm will stay up. You can't throw strikes consistently with your head up and the ball down, because you won't have good control. You have to keep your nose into the catcher's glove, and follow through with your arm straight to the target.

GLOSSARY

Backspin: The movement of a baseball that spins back in the opposite direction.

Changeup: A pitch that looks like a fastball but is slower.

Foul pole: The poles in left and right field that mark fair and foul territory.

Rubber: The rectangular slab in the middle of the pitcher's mound, where the pitcher stands.

Seams: The lines of stitching on a baseball.

Sink: Drop toward the ground as it reaches the plate.

Sprints: Running as fast as you can from one point to another.

Target: Where you want to throw the ball. For a pitcher, this is usually where the catcher places his mitt.

Truest flight: The straightest path toward the target.

Windup: The pitcher's motion when he delivers a pitch to the plate. Both feet are on the rubber and he faces the hitter head-on as he begins his delivery.

★★★★★★★★★★★★★★★★★★★★★★★★★★★★

EXTREMELY WELL ARMED!

Most pitchers have to make sure just one of their arms is especially stretched and loose for an appearance in a game.

But not Greg Harris.

Harris made big league history, pitching as both a right-hander and a left-hander in the same inning of a September 28, 1995, game at Montreal's Olympic Stadium. It was something that Harris had always wanted to do. He was ambidextrous, which means he was able to perform certain tasks, such as using a fork, equally well with each hand.

As a member of the Boston Red Sox, Harris pitched right-handed. But during batting practice, he would catch balls and throw them in from the outfield using his left arm. He had a rare six-finger glove that allowed him to use it on either hand. When Harris was traded to the Montreal Expos in 1995, his manager, Felipe Alou, decided it was time for an ambidextrous pitcher to appear in the big leagues.

The Cincinnati Reds were ahead of the Expos by six runs when Harris was called in to pitch the ninth inning. As a right-hander, he retired Reggie Sanders, a right-handed hitter, on a routine ground ball to shortstop.

Then the Reds had a couple of left-handed hitters come to the plate. Harris shifted positions and stood on the pitching rubber as a left-hander. His first left-handed pitch was wild and it sailed to the backstop. The next three weren't much better and he walked Hal Morris on four straight pitches.

But then Harris settled down. He retired the next batter, Ed Taubensee, on a tapper in front of the plate. Then, as a right-handed pitcher, he set down Bret Boone on a bouncer back to the mound. The big leagues' first ambidextrous pitcher didn't give up a single run!

HERE'S THE SITUATION

The sun is out, it's very hot, and you've been running around all day with your friends. Maybe you've even gone swimming.

You're tired, and you're pitching in a game that night.

You don't want to stretch.

Does the heat make you loose enough that you don't need to stretch before the game? Should you not warm up, figuring that the fewer pitches you throw, the longer you'll be able to pitch in the game?

HERE'S THE SOLUTION

Always stretch! No matter how warm the weather, and no matter how loose you feel, you still need to make sure your arm is fully stretched out. And remember to stretch your legs, too…even if they feel tired from your day with your friends.

As for warm-up pitches, maybe you can throw fewer because the heat is going to take its toll on your energy. You will probably get tired faster, so it's not a bad idea to conserve your efforts.

But remember, that's only if you've stretched out your arms and legs first!

★★★★★ MEMORIES ★★★★★

I played for Junction Insurance in the North Kittsap Little League, a small town in Poulsbo, Washington. Our uniforms were maroon and gray. We had maroon hats with a gray "JI" on them.

When I was 12 years old, we won the championship. I played with a lot of good guys who are still my friends today. I remember having a really, really fun time. After the games, we'd all go to the concessions stands for sodas and hot dogs. If we were really lucky, we got a candy bar or ice cream with our hot dogs.

We had three or four kids in one neighborhood that played on the same team. When we weren't playing for the team, we'd play stickball out in the vacant lots.

When I was 11, my dad, Galen, was my coach. He let me throw one curveball an inning. I think that was a good idea. Kids who are younger should throw just fastballs and **changeups,** because those pitches don't stress your arm like a curveball does. A curveball or a slider, if thrown improperly, can damage your arm.

The best way to throw a changeup is to make your thumb and index finger into a "C" and then stuff the ball in there. Throw it as hard as you can, like a fastball. But because the ball is not on the end of your fingers, it will come out soft.

When I was 12, I was allowed to throw two curveballs an inning. The coaches called the pitches for us, so I didn't have a chance to throw more than two.

I was a very fiery competitor back then. If I struck out, or if I threw a bad pitch, I would get upset. I'd get to the point where I wanted to throw my helmet. But if I slammed a bat on the ground, my dad would take me out of the game. It was the best thing that ever happened to me, because it taught me how to be a good sport.

Baseball is supposed to be fun. No matter what you think you should do, people will strike out, and people will have bad games pitching. Even Babe Ruth struck out every now and then. You want to be competitive, but you're also supposed to have a good time.

I think you can learn as much from failure as you can from success. You have to learn to handle failure. It can be tough sometimes, but you have to rebound on things and work harder. You might realize what you're doing isn't working. So you might need to try something different or you might have to work harder. Maybe you should even talk to a coach to learn more.

I've failed at times. But I always think to myself that I can get better, and that I'm going to practice so I can play better.

When you succeed, it's almost the opposite. You have to think, "What did I do right? And if I had success doing that, what would happen if I worked harder, or if I talked to my coach and learned more?"

You have to handle success the right way, too. Everyone is going to succeed at times and everyone is going to fail at times. Stay on a balanced level emotionally. And remember, it's all about having fun!

Photograph courtesy of Boston Red Sox

THE ART OF PITCHING

PEDRO MARTINEZ

No two pitchers throw exactly the same way. Either their pitching motions are different, or they might stand on a different place on the pitching **rubber,** or they may use their legs in a different fashion. But even though all pitchers throw in their own unique ways, there are some important lessons that every young pitcher should learn.

In this chapter, Cy Young Award winner Pedro Martinez talks about pitching mechanics.

How do you strengthen your arm?

I get my arm strong by playing **long toss.**

Long toss is throwing the ball a long way, from one corner of the outfield to another. But you should always throw according to your size. So if you're a Little Leaguer, you shouldn't throw as far as the big leaguers do. Try tossing the ball from center field to right field, or maybe from left field to center field.

When you're in the **windup** position on the mound, where do you put your feet?

I always put my feet right in the middle of the rubber. It's a rule in baseball that a pitcher must always be touching the rubber when he makes a pitch. So when I'm turning in my motion to the plate, the outside of my right foot goes along the inside part of the rubber. I dig a little hole in front of the rubber, so I can place my foot there when I'm in my motion. That helps prevent my foot from slipping.

Why do you stand in the middle of the rubber?

It helps with your control. Plus, the hitter can't tell if you're going to throw to the inside or outside corner of the plate. But if you have a hard time throwing to the inside or outside corners, you should try standing more to one side. For instance, if you have trouble throwing to the inside corner against a right-handed batter, then stand on the right side of the rubber. That might help you hit your spot.

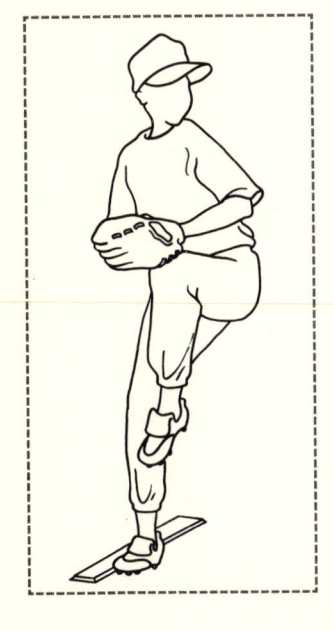

Instead of digging a hole for your foot, why not just throw with your foot on top of the rubber?

If you stand on top of the rubber, you will not get as good a push off the rubber, which will affect the strength of your pitch. Also, by placing your foot against the rubber, you are securing your foot so that it doesn't slide around. You don't want to slip when throwing the ball.

Why do you need the push off the rubber? How important is that?

This is going to sound a little weird, but the push from your legs helps your **velocity,** which is your speed on the ball. The push from your legs is probably half, or even 60 percent, of your strength on the mound.

If you have strong legs and you use them the right way, you will get really good velocity. And it all begins with the push off the rubber.

Is the push from the legs as important—or even more important—than the arm action?

Everything comes from the legs. That's why you have to make sure you strengthen your legs before you do any type of throwing.

When you throw a pitch, do you ever take your eye off the catcher's mitt?

I try to keep my eyes on the target all the way from the moment I start my **windup** to the point that the ball crosses home plate. I try not to move my head when I make my pitch.

Why is it important not to move your head during the delivery of a pitch?

The less you move your head, the better your control will be. It's hard to keep your head on the **target** all of the time. But if you can do it, it will help you throw a lot of strikes. It's very helpful for your control.

When did you learn the importance of keeping your head still?

I think it took me about three years in the big leagues. The sooner you learn to keep your head still, the better you will pitch.

How did you practice keeping your head still?

No, I didn't practice with a neck brace! I just concentrated on doing everything slowly. I tried not to overdo anything with my **mechanics,** my arm, and my body. You have to remember that you can't be too quick. Just let everything work out nice and slowly. And do things the same way with every pitch.

When you're practicing on the sidelines, getting ready to pitch in a game, what do you work on? Is pitching practice similar to batting practice?

Yes, it's pretty much the same. You practice and practice and practice throwing on the sidelines. Then you go into a game and do exactly what you just did in practice.

So you have to concentrate in practice as much as you do in a game?

Yes. If you don't, you're wasting time and effort.

How do you follow through when pitching from the windup?

The **follow-through** is really important. That's what saves your arm. Your muscles have to become fully extended when you make a pitch. If you don't follow through, or "finish," then you'll have **recoil.** Recoil is when your arm doesn't properly follow through. If you recoil, you're playing with fire. Your muscles will never become fully extended the way they should be, and you're risking injury.

When you pitch a baseball, you're pushing the muscles to throw the ball forward. So you want to keep your arm motion following through. If you don't, you're putting extra stress on the arm.

What do you mean by "finish?"

You want to follow the ball with your arm and body, and maybe take a step forward, once you release the ball. I don't finish forward with a step, but I do finish with my arm. My arm is extended to a position right beside my left leg. Think about the delivery of a right-handed pitcher, and then picture your right arm finishing up beside your left knee. That's what you want to do.

Where should a pitcher's eyes be?

Your eyes have to be looking at the target and the batter. Your focus helps with your location, and it also helps you to protect yourself. If you take your eyes off the ball, you can't see if the batter hits the ball back at you, and you won't be able to react.

How important is it for a pitcher to be balanced when he throws?

If you want to throw strikes, it's very important! If you're off balance, you won't be able to concentrate on your target nearly as well. And that means the ball won't go where you want it to.

GLOSSARY

Count: The number of balls and strikes the batter has on him during an at-bat. For instance, the count may be two balls and no strikes. Or it could be three balls and two strikes, which is called a full count.

Follow-through: Completing your arm movement after the ball is thrown, almost as if you were drawing a big circle with your arm.

Long toss: Playing catch at a long distance.

Mechanics: The body movements involved in pitching a baseball.

Recoil: The incorrect form after releasing a pitch, where the arm doesn't follow through with the pitch. Instead, the arm stops and pulls back a little, causing extra stress on the arm muscles.

Rubber: The rectangular slab in the middle of the pitcher's mound, where the pitcher stands.

Target: Where you want to throw the ball.

Velocity: The speed of a pitch. Using your legs correctly will help you to get better velocity on your pitches.

Windup: The pitcher's motion when he delivers a pitch to the plate. Both of his feet are on the rubber and he is facing the hitter head-on as he starts his delivery.

BLOWN AWAY!

Stu Miller was not the biggest pitcher in baseball history.

In fact, he stood a shade under 6 feet tall and weighed only 165 pounds. He was a relief pitcher in the major leagues for 16 seasons.

In 1961, the right-handed Miller was pitching so well for the San Francisco Giants that he was named to the National League's All-Star team for the first of two All-Star Games that year.

The date was July 11 and the game was being played at the Giants' home field, Candlestick Park.

It was always windy at Candlestick Park. Very windy. And on this particular day, the wind was unusually strong.

Miller entered the game in the top of the ninth inning. But as he began his windup to throw a pitch, a huge gust of wind literally blew him off the pitching rubber. He had to stop his motion to keep from falling over!

While that must have been a rather embarrassing moment for Stu Miller, he soon wound up claiming a more favorable All-Star distinction. Miller was the winning pitcher in the National League's 5–4 victory over the American League.

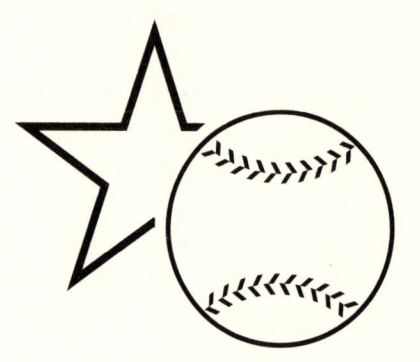

HERE'S THE SITUATION

The bases are loaded. The game is tied. It's the bottom of the final inning. There are two outs.

The batter coming to the plate is a good hitter.

Should you "nibble" with your pitches, and try to throw a strike over the outside corner of the plate? Or should you throw the ball over the middle and just see what happens?

HERE'S THE SOLUTION

There is no good option in this case.

If you try to throw the first couple of pitches over the corner and you miss, you're down in the **count** at two balls and no strikes. Now you're in danger of walking in the winning run. No one wants to lose on a bases-loaded walk. So in this case, it's probably better to throw the ball over the plate, even if it's down the middle.

If you make the batter hit the ball, one of your fielders has the chance to make a play. You just might get the batter to ground out to one of your infielders, or hit a lazy fly ball to the outfield. Then you're headed for extra innings and your team can still win the game.

So instead of nibbling, challenge the hitter. Make the batter hit the ball to beat you.

★★★★★ **MEMORIES** ★★★★★

I played in a couple of tournaments in the Dominican Republic, which is where I'm from. I actually did a pretty good job. I was chosen to represent my country in the Little League World Series, but I couldn't go because my parents couldn't afford to send me.

When I was a kid, I was a pitcher and an outfielder. I played for teams called the Royals, the Braves, and the Cubbies. I remember playing in the "big" field once, when I was 13. We were playing in the championship game, all tied up at three wins apiece. In the seventh and final inning, they had a pitcher who used to strike me out all the time. He threw a nasty curveball. Before I went up to the plate, I remember realizing that I stepped back every time I saw that pitcher's curveball. I was always sure it was going to hit me. And when I jumped back, the ball would be a strike. So when I went up to the plate this time, I decided to try to let the ball hit me and see what happened.

But instead of the ball hitting me, I hit a home run…in the big field! No one my age had ever hit it out there. That was probably the most enjoyable moment I had as a kid playing baseball.

As a pitcher, I overpowered everybody. I had the talent as a kid to throw hard, but I didn't throw no-hitters. During a championship game when I was 14 years old, I probably threw only 70 or 80 miles an hour, but I had a great **breaking ball.** I came in as a relief pitcher and the game lasted

14 innings. I threw 12 of them, and we finally won the game.

I also remember getting our butts kicked a lot when I was younger, too. Sometimes I'd get snappy...I didn't like to lose. I'd throw my glove and my shoes around. Our coach told us we had to learn how to win as well as how to lose. But I guess I didn't listen to my coach about that, because I still get snappy when I lose!

—*Pedro Martinez*

FIELDING
THE
POSITION

PAUL
QUANTRILL

Throwing the ball is only one part of a pitcher's job. He also has to become a fielder when the batter hits the ball in his direction. No matter how good a pitcher is, players will hit at least some of his pitches—and he must be ready to field the ball just like any other fielder.

In this chapter, All-Star Paul Quantrill discusses techniques for becoming a successful fielding pitcher.

How important is it for a pitcher to be a good fielder?

It's a vital part of the game. It can help your team win ballgames.

As a pitcher, your most important job is to make a good pitch to get the hitter out. Hopefully, you strike him out, or he doesn't hit the ball too hard. But as soon as the pitch leaves your hand, you must become an infielder. If you have a strong pitching form, you can land in a position that allows you to immediately field the ball.

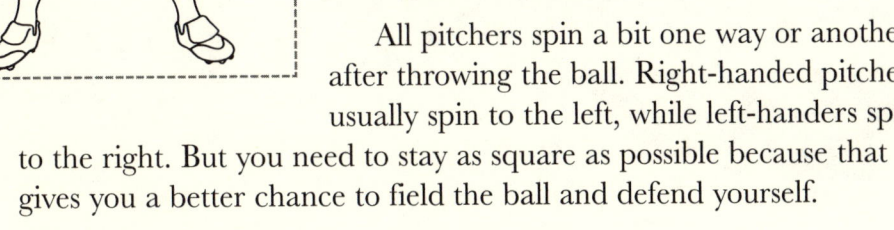

What is a good fielding position?

When you release the ball as a right-handed pitcher, you land on your left foot. After you throw the ball, you follow through and land on your right foot. Then you want to make sure you're **squared up,** which means that you're facing home plate.

Is it difficult to end up in a position facing home plate?

All pitchers spin a bit one way or another after throwing the ball. Right-handed pitchers usually spin to the left, while left-handers spin to the right. But you need to stay as square as possible because that gives you a better chance to field the ball and defend yourself.

What kind of things is a pitcher doing when he's "fielding the position?"

"Fielding the position" can mean anything from gobbling up baseballs hit back at you, to picking off runners, to covering first base on a double play, or even to covering first base on ground balls hit to the right side of the infield.

Why does a pitcher cover first base on ground balls hit to the right side?

On anything hit to the right side, a pitcher must move toward first base. It doesn't matter if you know it's a one-hopper that's heading right to the second baseman—you should still be busting over to first base to cover the bag. The reason for this is that you never know if the first baseman is going after the ball and whether he'll be able to cover first base in time.

How is fielding a ball as a pitcher different from the way another infielder might field a ball?

It's really no different. When you field your position as a pitcher, you catch the ball, set your feet, and then throw to first base—exactly as you would if you were a third baseman, second baseman, or short-stop.

How do you field a bunt?

The most important thing in fielding a bunt is having enough time to field the ball and make a throw to get a runner out. If you're falling over yourself or spinning off the mound so hard that your motion keeps you from squaring up, you won't be able to get to the ball in time.

There's really no reason not to get in decent fielding position for a bunt. As soon as you see the batter **square around,** you should get your momentum moving toward home plate.

Do you charge in as hard as you can when you see a batter square around?

No. After you release the ball and you see the batter square, you don't want to just take off. You should release the ball, get a little momentum going forward, and stay balanced by keeping your feet underneath you. Don't charge full on. Having your correct momentum going forward will help you react to the bunt, whether it's hit toward third base or first base, or even back to the mound.

Does it help to know how fast the batter bunting the ball can run?

That's the biggest mistake most pitchers make on bunts. You should always know how fast a batter runs. This will help you figure out how much time you have to pick up the ball and make a throw to first. If you know the runner isn't too fast, you know you don't have to rush your throw.

What does "rushing a throw" mean?

Basically, it means throwing the ball too quickly.

When you rush, you can't get your feet properly balanced, so you'll have less control over your throw. This can happen when a pitcher races over to grab a ball that's rolling down the third-base line. When he picks it up, his body momentum is falling away from first base. If you don't set yourself, and look at your target first, you might try to make the throw too quickly. Then what started off to be a little bunt becomes a double, because you threw the ball past the first baseman.

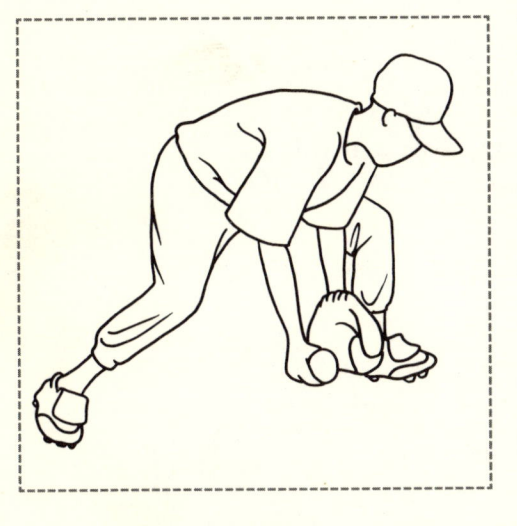

Do you use the glove or your bare hand to field a bunt?

If the ball is coming with some speed on it, you should use your glove. Make sure your bare hand is next to your glove. If you use two hands, it's much quicker to get the ball out of your glove to make the throw.

But if it's one of those bunts where you have to go to your **backhand** to field it—or if you had to knock the ball down because it was a hard bunt— always pick up the ball with your bare hand. That way, you'll be able to throw it twice as quickly.

On a very slow bunt, if you have big enough hands, if you have a good **read** on the ball, and if the ball's not bouncing around too much, using your bare hand is always quicker.

After fielding a grounder, what should you do to get a forceout at second base?

One thing you *shouldn't* do is turn and throw too quickly before your shortstop or second baseman has a chance to cover the bag. Slow yourself down a bit if your fielders aren't ready. If you've already started your throwing motion, assuming that someone will be there, you'll probably slow down your arm a bit to compensate. Then you'll end up lobbing the ball, or throwing it into center field by accident.

Year after year, we're taught to do a little **crow hop** in this situation. For a right-handed thrower, this means catching the ball in your glove as your left foot hits the ground. Next you do a little hop, pushing off the left foot and landing on your right. Then you should quickly push off your right foot and throw the ball, landing back on your left foot. Remember to keep your stride very short. If no one is covering the bag yet and you have the ball, you should take these short steps, keeping your momentum going toward the bag. When the fielder gets there, you can let the throw rip.

Does the second baseman or shortstop have to be standing on the bag when you make the throw?

No, a fielder doesn't have to be on second base when you throw. But he should be close enough so that, when you throw the ball, he's there in time to catch it.

Where should you throw the ball?

Chest high, right over the bag.

Always remember: If you're going for a double play, you have to make sure you get that **lead runner.** You can't get the second out on a double play until you get the first one.

What happens if your second baseman or shortstop forgets to cover the base? Or what if it looks as if the baserunner will beat a throw to second base?

Make sure to get at least one out. If you can't get a runner at second, then go for the easy out at first. I would probably turn and make a good throw to first for the easy out in this case.

How important is it to be balanced when you're making this kind of throw?

I can't stress it enough! The biggest mistake for pitchers is when they throw after fielding a ball without staying properly balanced. They'll be bending down, or on the move, or even running, trying to get the ball and throw it quickly to the base. And they'll usually be out of control. Now, there *are* cases when you simply have to throw this way to have any chance of getting the out. But more often than not, you've got a bit of time. So get your feet under you and get balanced.

Is there a certain body position that works best for throwing?

You want to be turning your body toward your target as you field the ball. That will put you in better position quicker, and you'll be able to throw to your target quicker as well.

What kind of throw should you make to first base after fielding a routine ground ball?

You don't need to throw too hard, but I'm also not big on a **lob** to first. Just take a step toward first base, and throw the ball normally. If you're so close to the first baseman that you're worried about throwing the ball too hard, then give him an **underhand toss.** I don't mean the kind of underhand toss that's used in softball pitching, where the toss is real high up in the air. Simply throw an easy **line drive** underhanded. It's quick and firm, and you should try to hit the first baseman in the chest, just like any other throw.

GLOSSARY

Backhand: Reaching across with the glove over the bare-hand side of the body.

Crow hop: A short, three-part move—similar to a dance step—players use to get their feet in a good position to make a strong throw.

Forceout: An "out" recorded by stepping on a base as opposed to having to tag the runner.

Lead runner: The baserunner who has advanced the farthest. For instance, if runners are at first and second, the lead runner is at second base.

Line drive: A ball thrown firmly without much arc.

Lob: A high, soft throw.

Read: An idea of where the ball will go.

Square around: The position a batter takes when he's about to bunt the ball. This involves either pivoting at the waist and moving the top hand up the bat as the pitch is delivered, or moving the back foot up and parallel to the front foot, so the batter is facing the pitcher.

Squared up: The best body position for a pitcher to be in after he makes a pitch. He's balanced directly facing the hitter.

Underhand toss: A throw where the palm of your hand is facing up toward the sky. It's generally a soft—but firm—toss.

★★★★★★★★★★★★★★★★★★★★★★★★★★

AN UNUSUAL TOSS!

Many pitchers can throw the ball at 90 miles per hour, or faster. And there are times when a batter will hit the ball back to the pitcher even faster. The pitcher's job is to flag down these missiles. If the ball is hit on the ground, the pitcher has to grab it and throw to first base. This is usually not too difficult, especially if a ball is hit softly. But one day, Orlando "El Duque" Hernandez of the New York Yankees got one of those fast missiles and it caused a slight problem.

Right-hander El Duque was pitching against the New York Mets on June 5, 1999, at Yankee Stadium. He was facing Rey Ordonez, who hit a bouncer toward him. El Duque reached out with his glove and caught the bouncer. The ball settled in the webbing of his glove. The pitcher's momentum took him toward first base. He took a few short, easy strides toward the bag and reached into his glove for the ball. But the ball was stuck in the webbing. It was stuck so tightly that El Duque was afraid he wouldn't be able to get the ball out in time to throw to first before Ordonez reached the bag.

So the pitcher did some fast thinking.

He yanked the glove off his left hand and tossed the *glove,* which still held the baseball, to his first baseman, Tino Martinez. A surprised Martinez caught the glove. Since the ball was secure inside the glove, and since the glove arrived before Ordonez did, Ordonez was called out.

It was just your basic pitcher-to-first-baseman ground ball out, if you were scoring the play. But credit El Duque with some quick, creative problem-solving skills in order to get the out!

HERE'S THE SITUATION

The bases are loaded. You're pitching and your team is ahead by one run. It's the last inning. There's only one out. A ground ball is hit back to you at the mound. You field it cleanly.

Should you turn to throw to second base to start a double play? Or should you throw home to stop the tying run from scoring?

★ ★ ★ ★ ★ ★ ★ ★ ★ ★ ★ ★ ★ ★ ★ ★ ★

HERE'S THE SOLUTION

Go home!

If you throw to second base and you're not able to turn the double play, the tying run will score. Yes, you might be able to get the double play, but it's by no means a sure thing.

The throw home is much more of a sure thing. If you make a good throw and the catcher steps on home plate, you have the forceout. The tying run has not scored. Now you have two outs and you still have a forceout possibility at every base. Plus, if everything goes smoothly, the catcher might have time to throw to first base for a potential game-ending double play.

★★★★★ MEMORIES ★★★★★

I grew up in Port Hope, which is just east of Toronto, in Canada.

Hockey is the Canadian national sport. In Canada, every kid's baseball glove has puck marks on it. When you play goalie in street hockey, you put on all the equipment and guys blast pucks at you. Then your nice, brand-new Wilson A-2000 or your Rawlings or whatever glove you have always ends up with a bunch of black scuff marks on it.

I was mostly into hockey, but I played a lot of baseball when I was a kid. I started when I was about 7 or 8 years old. I was always in love with baseball. I always had a great time going out and playing with friends. And the game started to become easy for me. I could play catch all day long. The more I played, the better I got.

We had a town recreation league. Legion posts sponsored teams. I played for Garden Hill. My dad was one of the coaches. I remember absolutely loving it.

I also did pretty well, so they moved me up an age level with the big kids. I got my butt kicked on a daily basis as a pitcher. The kids were bigger, stronger, and faster than I was. But it made me compete and try to become a better player.

The thing about baseball is that I didn't take the game too seriously when I was a kid. And I don't think any kid should. They should just play and have a good time. It's the greatest sport, because there are so many different parts to it—hitting, fielding, and throwing—and all of those parts can be so much fun.

I never threw a breaking ball when I was a kid. You really don't need to throw that pitch until you get older. I played with some kids who had the same arm strength as I did, or close to it. It was neat to see them throw breaking balls. But by the time they were 14 or 15, their arms were hurting, while I was still throwing and having fun.

In addition to a fastball, I threw some changeups. They weren't very good at the time, but it was better for my arm than throwing breaking balls. Young pitchers should remember that breaking balls wear a young person's arm out.

Paul Quantrill

PART 2

CATCHING

THROWING OUT BASE-STEALERS

IVAN "PUDGE" RODRIGUEZ

The pitch is thrown and the runner on first base takes off for second. He is trying to steal the base. The catcher gets the ball and throws to second to try and nail the runner. But it takes more than just a strong arm to strike down an enemy basestealer.

In this chapter, MVP catcher Ivan "Pudge" Rodriguez talks about the skills that are needed to throw out baserunners.

When the bases are empty, what's the best way to catch a pitch?

I always want to feel as comfortable as I can behind the plate. When I catch the ball with no one on base, I put my bare hand behind my back. The more protection you have from a **foul tip,** the better. But if that doesn't work for you, then try something else. You should always catch the way in which you feel most comfortable.

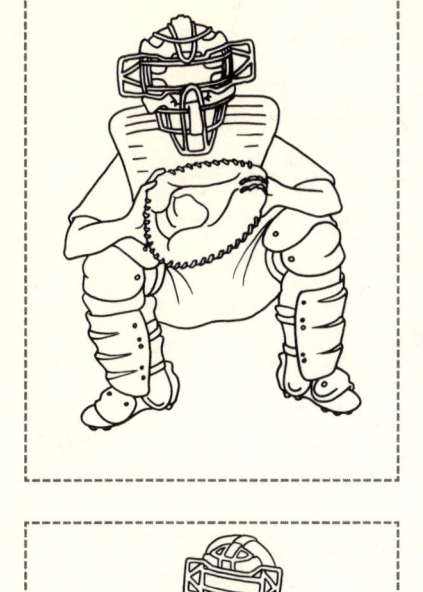

If there's a runner on base and he tries to steal, does the position of your hands change?

When there are guys on base, I always put my right hand just behind my glove. That way, I have a better chance to get the ball from my glove to my throwing hand quicker.

Do you make any changes in your stance when there's a baserunner and you think he might try to steal?

Yes, I spread my legs slightly wider apart. I stand up a bit more, too. I'm still squatting behind the plate, but I stand up just a little. That helps me get the ball to my throwing hand quicker.

How important are the catcher's feet when he's trying to throw out a base-stealer?

If you have a strong arm, you have a big advantage for throwing guys out. But if you don't have a strong arm, it really helps to have quick legs, so you can get into a good throwing position faster. The key is to always make a quick, accurate throw.

It doesn't really matter where you put your feet when the pitcher delivers the ball. You just have to be as comfortable as possible. But you should move your feet into position to throw just as you catch the ball.

What is the best arm angle for the throw?

I try to throw the ball over the top of my shoulder. If you throw it that way, the ball will carry toward the base better and you'll have the

40

chance to make a stronger throw. Your throw will be more accurate, too.

What happens if you throw from more of a **sidearm angle?**

The ball won't carry straight to the base. It will have some movement on it that will make it more like a **sinker.** The sidearm angle is usually not as effective in throwing out baserunners, because the ball can sail away from the target.

When you throw right-handed, is your left foot pointed at the base?

You want to point your left foot wherever you're going to throw the ball. If you're throwing to second base, then point your left foot toward second base. If you're throwing to third base, point your left foot to third base. That will improve your accuracy.

How important is the follow-through?

After you throw the ball, you should follow the ball with your arm. You shouldn't try to stop your arm once you let go of the ball. If you do, you could injure yourself. Let your arm go with the throw.

What kind of drills can a young catcher do to become quicker with his feet and hands?

If you want to increase your quickness, get a ball and find a wall somewhere. Throw the ball off the wall and catch it. Just throw and catch, throw and catch. Make sure to practice a good throwing position.

Are the mechanics of throwing out a basestealer at third base any different than second base?

No. It's the same process as throwing to second base. The only difference is that your left foot is pointing at third base instead of at second.

GLOSSARY

Arm angle: The position of your arm as you throw the ball.

Follow-through: Completing your arm movement after the ball is thrown, almost as if you were drawing a big circle with your arm.

Foul tip: A ball barely hit by the batter that generally strikes the catcher.

Lead runner: The baserunner that has advanced the farthest. For instance, if runners are at first and second, the lead runner is at second base.

Mechanics: The body movements involved in throwing a baseball.

Sidearm: A throwing motion in which the arm is about waist-high and parallel to the ground when releasing the ball.

Sinker: A throw in which the ball dips down toward the ground as it reaches the plate.

Stance: Your body position as the ball is pitched. A catcher's stance is called a squat. He crouches down with his knees bent, legs spread, and body as low as possible, while remaining completely balanced.

HEADS UP!

On May 12, 1967, the Detroit Tigers' Al Kaline took his lead from first base. Jon Wyatt was pitching for the Red Sox and Bob Tillman was the catcher.

On Wyatt's second pitch to the batter, Kaline broke for second, attempting to steal. Tillman caught the pitch and then fired a throw to second base. Wyatt turned his head toward second base to see what would happen.

But Tillman's throw was low. It smacked Wyatt on the back of the head, knocking the pitcher to the ground. The ball rolled to the on-deck circle between home plate and the first-base dugout. Kaline made it all the way to third base before the ball was picked up

Fortunately, Wyatt wasn't badly hurt. He had a headache, but he stayed in the game. On the next pitch, the batter hit a sacrifice fly off Wyatt, driving in Kaline for the winning run in the Tigers' 5–4 victory over the Red Sox.

HERE'S THE SITUATION

The other team has runners at first and second and there are two outs. The runner at second base has very good speed. But the runner at first base is not very fast at all. The pitch comes in. It's an easy one to catch. Both runners take off. It's a double steal.

As the catcher, you now have to make a decision. Do you throw to third base, trying to get the **lead runner**? Or do you throw to second base, knowing that the runner from first base doesn't have great speed?

HERE'S THE SOLUTION

Throw to second!

If you get an out, the inning is over. The pitch is an easy one to handle, so you should throw to the base where you have the best chance for success. In this case, it's second base, because the runner from first is slower than the runner from second.

But remember, there's one important thing you have to do as a catcher. You always have to anticipate what might happen. If you think the other team might try a double steal, you must let your infielders know, through a sign, which base you will be throwing to. That way, you'll make sure they cover the bag.

★ ★ ★ ★ ★ **MEMORIES** ★ ★ ★ ★ ★

I started playing baseball when I was 7 years old. I enjoyed the game a lot in Little League and all the leagues I played in. I learned a lot from all my coaches.

I grew up in Vega Baja, Puerto Rico. I played catcher, third base, second base, and pitcher. I played every position. I guess every kid likes to play every position when they're in Little League!

I was a pretty good hitter, but I just tried to do everything well. It was a lot of fun.

—*Ivan "Pudge" Rodriguez*

FOUL POP-UPS

JOHN FLAHERTY

It looks so easy. The ball is fouled by the batter and it floats high in the air, right around home plate. The catcher has such a big glove. How could he possibly miss? Well, nothing is ever as easy as it looks...and that goes for foul pop-ups, too.

In this chapter, defensive whiz John Flaherty talks about the do's and don'ts of catching foul pop-ups—so you can make sure that what goes up comes down in your mitt!

When the batter hits a foul pop-up, what's the first thing a catcher has to do?

Obviously, the first thing is to find the ball. To do that, you should take your mask off.

What do you do with the mask?

You want to make sure to hold onto your mask with your throwing hand. You don't want to let the mask just fall to the ground, because you might not know exactly where it is. And when you're chasing down a pop-up, you could trip over it and twist an ankle.

How do you chase the pop-up?

You should always remember that a pop-up behind home plate in foul territory is going to come back toward the field, because of the spin when it comes off the bat. To prepare for this, the catcher should turn his back to the field. That way, he'll be better prepared to handle the spin on the ball, with an easier angle to make the catch.

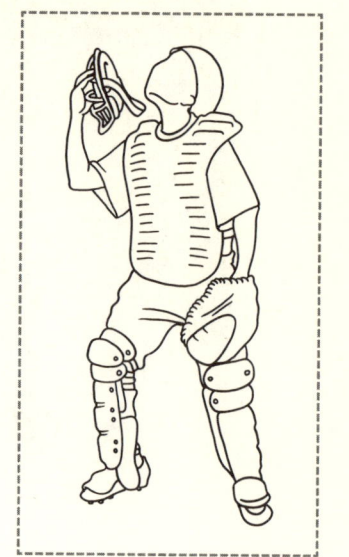

Shouldn't you be right under the ball to catch it, the same way an outfielder would catch a fly ball or an infielder would catch a pop-up?

No. If you do get right under it, the **backspin** on the ball will take it over your head, and you'll end up trying to backpedal to catch it. It's tough to catch the ball that way. So give yourself some room to play the backspin, so that the ball will come down to you, not over your head.

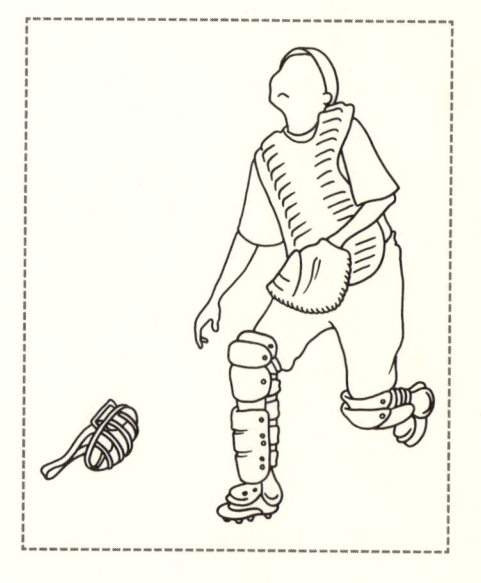

Do you catch the ball while you're still holding your mask?

Once you spot the ball and have a good idea of where the ball will eventually end up, then you can release your mask.

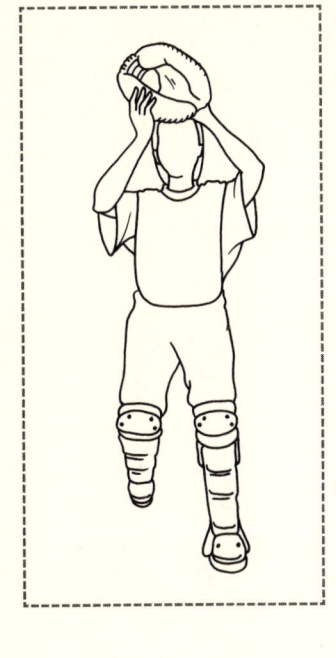

You said you don't want to drop the mask at your feet, so what do you do with it?

You don't have to throw it 30 feet away. But you do want to make sure to get it out of the way of where the ball will end up. Usually, a good 10 to 15 foot toss will do.

How do you catch a ball with that big catcher's mitt?

It's not always easy! But you want to try to receive the ball at the highest point possible. That way, you'll leave yourself a little room for error.

A lot depends on the height of the ball and its **velocity.** You want to catch it with your glove up, and the pocket of the glove facing toward the sky. You also want your throwing hand right next to the glove, so if you bobble the ball a bit, you'll have a chance to recover and still grab it before it hits the ground. It's a tougher play than most people think.

Suppose the pop-up isn't right over the plate?

If the ball isn't right at home plate, the catcher becomes a fielder, and he has to run after the ball. He should try to get to the spot he thinks the ball will land, in the most relaxed manner he can.

How do you run after the ball?

If you're trying to catch a ball on the run, make sure to run on the balls of your feet. That way, your head won't be bobbing and shaking. If your head is moving around, the ball will look as if it's moving around, too. That will make it harder to catch.

Do you keep your eye on the ball at all times?

The only time I take my eye off the ball is if the sun gets in my way, or if there's a play that will be close to the stands. If it's close to the stands, I might look over to see how much room I have left. Then I'll look back up to find the ball again. But those types of plays are few and far between.

GLOSSARY

Backspin: The movement of a baseball that spins back in the opposite direction from which it is hit. Sometimes it's difficult for a catcher to field a pop-up that has backspin on it.

Changeup: A pitch that looks like a fastball but is slower.

Opposite field: For a right-handed hitter, the opposite field would be right field. For a left-handed batter, it would mean the left side of the field.

Pulled: For a right-handed batter, this means hitting the ball to the left side of the field. For a left-handed batter, it means hitting the ball to the right side of the field.

Velocity: The speed.

★★★★★★★★★★★★★★★★★★★★★★★★★★★★

PETEY ON THE SPOT!

The Philadelphia Phillies' first World Series title was so close that the team and their fans at Veterans Stadium could almost taste victory. On October 21, 1980, the Phillies had a three-run lead in the top of the ninth inning. Philadelphia also had a three-games-to-two lead over the Kansas City Royals in the best-of-seven series.

But the Royals began to rally against Philadelphia left-hander Tug McGraw. A one-out walk and then back-to-back singles filled the bases, bringing Frank White to the plate. McGraw threw a pitch, and White lofted it foul. The ball drifted toward the Phillies' dugout, along the first-base line. Philadelphia catcher Bob Boone, one of the best defensive catchers to ever play the game, gave chase. He spotted the ball, tossed aside his mask and moved over to the dugout in pursuit.

As he did so, first baseman Pete Rose also raced in to give chase. If Boone couldn't get to the ball, Rose must have figured, maybe he'd be in position to grab it. Boone got to the ball and reached out with his mitt. The ball hit his mitt, but Boone didn't catch it cleanly. The ball hopped up into the air, and looked as if it would fall to the turf. But Rose was close enough to save the day. He reached out with his glove, and plucked the ball out of the air before it hit the ground. The Phillies got the out!

It was the second out of the inning. The Royals still had the bases loaded, but McGraw struck out the next Kansas City hitter, Willie Wilson, for the final out. The Phillies won the game and their first World Championship!

HERE'S THE SITUATION

There's a runner at third base and only one out. The batter lifts a high foul pop-up, near the first-base dugout. You quickly rip off your mask, holding it in your hand. You spot the ball and start to run over to the first-base dugout. You toss away your mask, get under the ball, and make the catch.

What do you do next?

HERE'S THE SOLUTION

After you've made the catch, you can't start snoozing. Unless there are three outs, there's always another play to make. In this case, after you've made the catch, the runner at third base could tag up and score. So after making the catch, you must quickly turn and check to see what the runner is doing. If the runner has tagged and is running home, you'll be ready to throw to the plate.

This is where teamwork comes into play. Obviously, you can't cover the plate yourself, because you had to make the catch near the first-base dugout. Either the third baseman or the pitcher should be covering the plate.

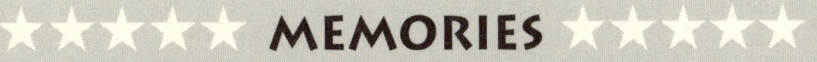

★ ★ ★ ★ ★ MEMORIES ★ ★ ★ ★ ★

The first baseball memory I can think of is when I was 12 years old. My team went 25–0 and won the Tournament of Champions in Rockland County, New York. It was a tournament for all the winners of their respective leagues, and the games raised money for disabled kids.

I had played as a 10-, 11-, and 12-year-old on the same team, the West Nyack Twins. We had won our league 3 years in a row, and we went to this tournament three years in a row, too. We won it when I was 12.

I have great memories of just wearing the uniform the whole day before a game. I couldn't wait to get out there and play, so I'd put on the uniform as soon as I woke up. I had a great Little League coach named Rich Cesca, who is still a good friend of mine today. There were practices I didn't want to go to, but he made sure I was there. He taught me a strong work ethic at a young age.

I was a catcher when I was 10 and 11. When I was 12, I pitched, and played first base. I'm bragging a little here, but I threw 8 no-hitters and only gave up 6 hits the whole year during the regular season. I had a tougher time pitching when we went to the tournament, where the overall competition was better, but that's another story!

When I pitched, I threw mostly fastballs. I was allowed to throw 6 curveballs a game. No more than that. And I made sure I got my six curveballs in every time. I would throw them to the best hitters, saving them for when I needed a big out. I didn't throw **changeups,** but that's what

I'd recommend now for kids. Fastballs and changeups are better for a young arm.

I wound up with a pain in my elbow that caused me to shut down my pitching career. So I went back behind the plate, and became a catcher again. The pain in my elbow was because I threw too many curveballs...and I only threw six a game! Kids should stick with fastballs and changeups, and only start throwing curveballs and sliders when they're older and their bodies can handle it better.

I hit two home runs when I was 12. I remember them like it was yesterday. One was a grand slam that I **pulled** to left field. I actually went to the **opposite field** (right field) for the other homer. I don't think I've hit an opposite-field homer since!

John Flhott

BLOCKING PITCHES IN THE DIRT

Photograph courtesy of Boston Red Sox

JASON VARITEK

There is no glamour in blocking pitches in the dirt. And sometimes it hurts. But as a catcher, you can't let a bad pitch bounce away with runners on base, if you can help it.

In this chapter, former College Player of the Year and U.S. Olympian Jason Varitek discusses the best body position for blocking pitches in the dirt.

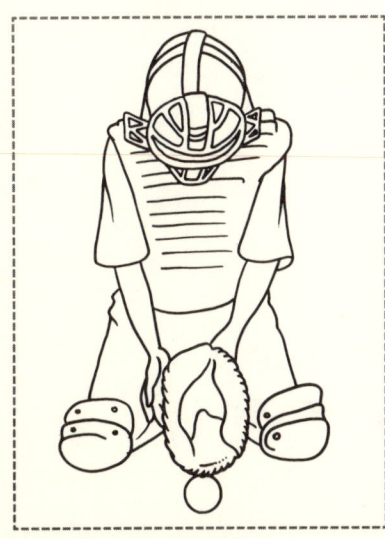

What is the first thing a catcher should do to block a ball in the dirt?

The first thing is to anticipate where the ball will go. You should expect the ball to be in the dirt every time, because that will help you be ready when it happens. You'll be in the proper position to keep the ball in front of you.

Anticipation is the first step. The next step is reaction.

54

What's the best body position for blocking balls?

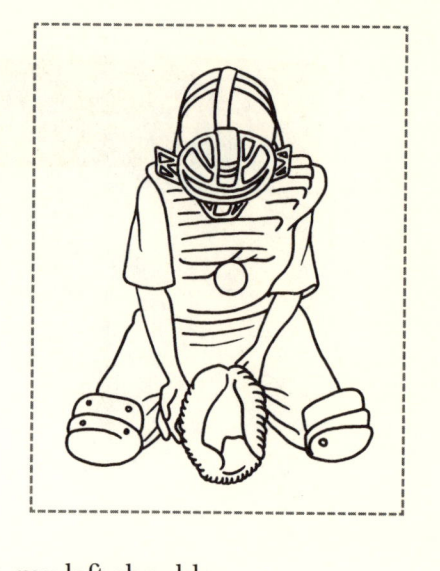

I try to make the ball hit me in the middle of my chest protector. Wherever the ball is—if it's to my right or left—I make sure I'm angled so that the ball will hit me, and bounce right back in front of the plate. Then I can recover the ball faster, so the runner won't have enough time to move up a base.

The type of pitch determines what your body angle should be. For instance, a **breaking ball** coming down from a right-handed pitcher is going to bounce back to my left because of the spin on the ball. In that case, my left shoulder should be turned inside, so it pushes the ball back to the plate.

I also try to keep my body as low as possible. If my chest is low to the ground and the ball bounces up and hits me, I can **deaden** the ball in front of me so I can reach it more easily. Leaning over at about a 45-degree angle works well.

Where are your hands?

Your glove and bare hand should block the space between your legs. Your bare hand should be underneath your glove and your elbows should be outside your legs. To help prevent injury, keep your hand in a loose fist so that your fingers are not spread out.

Where are your feet?

Your feet are behind your knees as you lean forward at a 45-degree angle. Your shoelaces are touching the ground. Basically, you want your feet out to the side, your knees and butt to the ground, and your hands blocking the space between your legs. Your elbows are positioned outside your hips, your chest is bent over at about a 45-degree

angle, and your shoulders should be rolled forward to deaden the ball. Keep your whole upper body relaxed.

Do you reach for a ball with your glove?

There's only so far you can move to each side.

You always want to slide your body over to where the ball is to get in front of it, because that helps keep the baserunner from advancing. But sometimes you just can't get out there. In that case, you have to reach. It really comes down to doing anything you possibly can to keep the ball from getting past you.

What's the best way to practice this important skill?

Repetition—practicing it over and over again. Find out which is your weak side, and which is your strong side. Figure out how to anticipate what types of pitches will bounce which ways.

How will a fastball react when it hits the dirt? What will other pitches do?

Straight fastballs tend to bounce straight back. Curveballs tend to bounce back toward the direction from which they were thrown. In the big leagues, pitchers throw other types of pitches, too. **Sliders** and **changeups** have a tendency to skid. **Forkballs** and split-finger fastballs generally have a mind of their own, so you don't really know where they'll go.

Where is your head positioned when blocking a ball in the dirt?

Your chin should be resting on your chest. That protects your throat. You always want your head over the ball. If you raise your head a little, the ball might hit you in the throat. If you turn your head to one side or the other, you might get the ball in your ear.

GLOSSARY

Breaking ball: A ball with a lot of spin. The most common type of breaking ball is a curveball.

Changeup: A pitch that looks like a fastball but is slower.

Deaden: Stop the ball from bouncing.

Forkball: A type of changeup in which the ball dips sharply as it approaches the plate.

Slider: A pitch thrown hard that has a small, sharp late break.

ONE THAT GOT AWAY!

Not much got past Mickey Owen. He was the best defensive catcher in the National League in 1941, starring for the Brooklyn Dodgers before they moved to Los Angeles. Owen set a league record that year. He handled 476 consecutive chances without an error. Over the course of the season, he compiled a .995 fielding position, which was a Dodgers record. But in the 1941 World Series against the New York Yankees, Owen was unable to hang onto a pitch from Hugh Casey. And that miscue helped the Yanks win the World Championship.

Up until that fateful moment in Game 4 at the Dodgers' Ebbetts Field, it looked as if Brooklyn was on the verge of tying the Series at two games apiece. With two outs in the top of the ninth, Casey and the Dodgers were one strike away from a 4–3 win. But the pitch that Casey threw to Tommy Henrich dipped away from Owen.

He couldn't catch strike three.

The ball got past him, and Henrich made it safely to first base.

The Yankees promptly made Owen and the Dodgers pay for the extra out. New York scored four runs after the miscue and won the game, 7–4. That gave the Yankees a 3–1 lead in the series, and the next day, New York notched the Series-clinching victory by a 3–1 score.

The Dodgers didn't make it back to the World Series until 1947, and didn't win a World Championship until 1955, in their eighth Series appearance.

HERE'S THE SITUATION

Runners are at first and third, with two outs. Your team is ahead by one run in the last inning. The pitcher delivers a ball in the dirt. You manage to block it. The ball doesn't get past you, but it squirts away a few feet in front of you. You scramble and quickly retrieve the ball. The runner at third starts down the line. But he sees the ball is still in front of you, so he decides to head back toward third.

The runner at first takes off for second base when the ball bounces away from you. Should you try to throw him out at second?

HERE'S THE SOLUTION

Many thoughts might be passing through your mind as you grab the ball and look up to see what's happening. How fast is the runner moving toward second base? Is an infielder covering second? How good a grip do you have on the ball? How far down the third-base line is the runner from third? If you throw to second, will the runner from third break for home?

There's only one way you should make the throw to second in this case: if you are 100 percent positive that you can throw the runner out at second base. If you're not 100 percent certain, then hold onto the baseball. Don't throw it. You'll still be up one run, and you're still one pitch away from winning the game.

Now, if you were ahead by six runs and there were two outs in the final inning, you might take a shot at throwing out the runner trying for second. If it doesn't work, and the runner from third scores on the play, it's not that big a deal…you're still up five runs. But with two outs in a close game, it's not worth the risk.

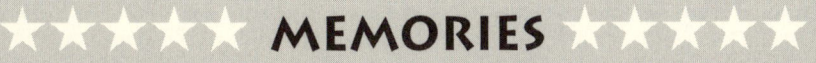

★★★★★ MEMORIES ★★★★★

I have a huge Little League memory that stands out from the rest. I got to play in the Little League World Series in Williamsport, Pennsylvania, in 1984. I was playing for Altamonte Springs, Florida.

We won all our games, so we got the chance to play on national television for a world championship. I was 12, and it was a pretty neat experience.

We lost 6–2 to Seoul, South Korea. It was the only game we lost all summer in the tournaments. We had won 17 or 18 games before that. But it was really fun. I was 12 years old, and I was signing autographs! We got to meet Baseball Hall of Famers like Willie Stargell and Jim Palmer. Willie threw out the first pitch and Jim broadcast the game. It was really a great experience.

I caught and played shortstop for my team. I didn't get a hit that day against South Korea. I actually didn't hit very well in Williamsport. But I did do well in the district, regional, and state tournaments. I hit around 8 to 10 home runs. I'm a switch-hitter now, which means I can bat both right-handed and left-handed. But I was just a right-handed hitter then.

I always keep an eye out for the Little League World Series championship game when it's on TV every summer. It brings back nothing but good memories for me.

Jason A. Varitek

PART 3

INFIELD

Photograph courtesy of the Cincinnati Reds

FIRST BASE

SEAN CASEY

T he first baseman is usually very active during the course of a game. He makes throws. He fields ground balls. He catches throws from other infielders.

In this chapter, All-Star Sean Casey talks about what it takes to play a strong first base.

What is a good position for a first baseman as a ball is pitched?

You always have to be ready. Make sure that you're on your toes instead of being flat-footed. You're more ready to move to where the ball is hit when you're on your toes.

What about your hands and arms?

You can have your hands wherever they feel comfortable, because you don't want your body to be tight. Make sure your body is loose and relaxed, but be ready for action at any time. Your arms can hang down in front of you, or just wherever they hang when they're loose.

When a ground ball comes to you, where do you want to catch it?

You want to field the ball out in front of you. Make sure you get your butt down so you can get your glove in front. If you do this, you'll have your body tilted forward, ready to make a play. Also, your head should always be down so you can watch the ball.

Is fielding a ground ball as a first baseman the same as fielding one as a third baseman, shortstop, or second baseman?

It's a little different. A first baseman does not make long throws after grabbing the ball. Usually, after fielding a ground ball, you either make a flip to the pitcher covering first base, or you take the ball yourself, run over, and step on the bag for the out.

How important is it to get in front of the ball when you're fielding it?

You definitely want to play the ball in front of you. That way, if it takes a **bad hop,** it will hit off your chest and drop in front of you. Then you can recover, pick up the ball, and step on the base.

What about the times when you have to make a throw after fielding a ground ball? How do you do that?

If you're throwing to second base to start a double play, for instance, set your feet to make sure you're making an accurate throw. On a ball that's hit right at you, you should act almost like a second baseman and **pivot** to make a throw to the base. Shuffle your feet a little after you field the ball, so you can turn and make a good throw.

If the ball is hit slightly to your left, field it in front of you. If you're a right-handed first baseman, spin around to your left and throw to second.

When a ground ball is not hit to you, what do you do?

When you see a ground ball hit somewhere else, your main objective is to get to first base.

How quickly do you have to get to the base?

You want to **sprint** to the bag, not jog. Get to the bag as quickly as you can, find the base with your feet, and then turn to the infield. When you're running to the bag, you already know where the ball has been hit. So when you get to the base, turn to where the ball was hit and pick up your **target.** As soon as you reach the bag, look up.

Where do you put your feet when you're covering the base?

I like to put one foot on each of the infield corners of the base. This helps me make my **read** on the ball when it's thrown. I see where the ball is headed, and then position myself toward it in order to catch the ball.

Do you stretch out for the ball right away?

You never want to stretch out too soon. You want to see where the ball is first. If the ball is headed a little to your left, place your foot on the inside corner, the one closest to home plate. If the throw is to your right, put your foot on the other corner. Then stretch for the ball.

If you stretch too soon, you won't be able to react as well to where the ball was thrown. Always set yourself up to cover the largest possible area.

Which foot do you put on the bag?

If you are a right-handed first baseman, always put your right foot on the bag and stretch out with your left foot on a routine grounder. If you're a left-handed first baseman, do the opposite.

How do you scoop up throws in the dirt?

I was always taught that you have to be aggressive. Go get the ball rather than sit back on it. If you sit back, the ball is going to **beat you.**

You also have to read the hop. If it's a **long hop,** you can be a little softer with your hands. You can see the hop and then wait for the bounce. But if you see that the ball is going to hit just several inches in front of you, you need to go get the ball on a **short hop** to make it easier to grab.

How do you pick up a ball on the short hop?

You keep your glove on a low plane, almost sweeping it along the ground. Don't sweep up with your glove.

How does a first baseman play a bunt? Charge in? Stay back to cover the base?

Again, you have to be aggressive, but you also have to use good judgment. If the ball looks like it's stopping at the pitcher's mound or right in front of home plate, you shouldn't run in without making a read. If you think it would be an easier play for you to make than anybody else, then run in there. But if you think someone else has an easier chance on it, stay back and cover the bag. It's really a judgment call.

GLOSSARY

Bad hop: A ball that doesn't bounce in a predictable manner. It may unexpectedly bounce to the left or right or even up high.

Beat you: Get past you.

Forceout: An "out" recorded by stepping on a base as opposed to having to tag the runner.

Lead runner: The baserunner who has advanced the farthest. For instance, if runners are at first and second, the lead runner is at second base.

Long hop: A bounce that occurs a long distance away from the fielder.

Pivot: Twist your body to face the target for your throw.

Read: An idea of where the ball will go.

Short hop: A bounce close to the fielder. It is just enough out of reach so that he can't catch the ball with his glove before it hits the ground.

Sprint: Run as fast as you can from one point to another.

Target: Where the ball is coming from.

★★★★★★★★★★★★★★★★★★★★★★★★★

A LAPSE AT FIRST THAT WAS SECOND TO NONE

Bill Buckner was a very good player. He hit the ball well and was a solid first baseman. Above all, he was a warrior—someone who played hard despite painful injuries. Buckner had bad ankles that required medical treatment before and after each game. He was a guy you'd always want to have on your team.

Unfortunately for Bill Buckner, though, he will forever be remembered for one play he didn't make: a ground ball hit by the New York Mets' Mookie Wilson against the Boston Red Sox in Game 6 of the 1986 World Series. Buckner's misplay in the tenth inning came in full view of 55,078 fans at Shea Stadium, as well as a national television audience. And it came after the Red Sox had squandered a chance to win their first World Series title since 1918.

Boston was leading the best-of-seven Series, three games to two. The Red Sox had broken a tie and taken a 5–3 lead in the top of the tenth inning. All that was standing in the way of the Sox and their long-coveted World Championship was three outs in the bottom of the tenth. And their reliever, Calvin Schiraldi, got the first two batters out.

With one out left in the game, Gary Carter singled. So did Kevin Mitchell. And then Ray Knight singled, driving in Carter and sending Mitchell to third base. The next batter, Mookie Wilson, watched a wild pitch from

★★★★★★★★★★★★★★★★★★★★★★★★★★★★★★★

Bob Stanley come flying past him and the catcher Rich Gedman. This allowed Mitchell to score the tying run. Then, on a 3–2 pitch, Wilson hit a slow roller down the first-base line. Buckner moved over to his left to field the ball. But he didn't get his glove down low enough. The ball rolled between Buckner's legs and into right field for an error. Knight scored easily, giving the Mets an amazing 6–5 win that tied the World Series at three games apiece.

In Game 7, the Red Sox coughed up an early three-run lead in an 8–5 loss as the New York Mets captured the World Championship.

HERE'S THE SITUATION

You're playing first base. There's a runner at first and one out. The batter hits a ground ball toward the line, not far from the first-base bag. You move to your left and grab the grounder. You know you want to get the double play. But when you field the grounder, you're not sure what to do.

Should you tag the first-base bag and then throw to second base? Or should you spin around and throw to second base and then rush back to cover first for the return throw?

HERE'S THE SOLUTION

You have to make a quick decision. If you're more than a couple of steps from the bag, your best option is to spin around and make the throw to second for the **forceout.** That way, if you don't end up getting the second out at first base, at least you've cut down the **lead runner.** And if the relay back to you is in time, then you have your double play. But if you feel your body's momentum is taking you toward first base as you field the ball, it's better to step on the bag for the first out and then throw to second, where the fielder would have to tag the runner for the second out on the play. If the first baseman steps on the bag for the first out, the force at second base is removed, making it necessary to tag the runner for the second out of the double play.

★ ★ ★ ★ ★ **MEMORIES** ★ ★ ★ ★ ★

I grew up in Upper St. Clair, Pennsylvania, which is a little suburb just south of Pittsburgh.

I played for a bunch of Little League teams. I really enjoyed those days. Looking back, the most fun summer I had was when I was 12 years old and I was traveling on an all-star team.

I remember winning the Home Run King trophy in the Robinson Township Tournament. I hit two home runs, the most in the tournament. That was kind of neat. I still have the trophy. And we won the tournament, too.

Our team was really good. We were in 6 or 7 tournaments and won 5 of them. We always had good teams. Dave Klasnick was our coach. He loved baseball, so he taught us all the lingo and a few other things. We had an assistant coach, Rob D'Onofrio, who had a big van. It wasn't a minivan, but it had a TV in it. We used to pile in and sing songs like Lionel Ritchie's "Dancing on the Ceiling." Those were some good times.

I played first and pitched. I was one of the bigger kids. When I was 12, I hit around .560 with about 12 homers. Our whole team hit well. When we were in the Robinson Township Tournament, there was a kid named Tim Garvey who hit a bomb off the scoreboard. Everyone said, "Wow, he hit the scoreboard. That's awesome!" I was the next hitter up, and I hit one over the scoreboard. It was probably 210 feet away, but that was a pretty far shot back in those days.

I used a 31-inch, 24- to 25-ounce bat. We all used the same bat. It had some serious dents in it by the end of the year!

SECOND BASE

JERRY HAIRSTON JR.

The second baseman doesn't have to make many long throws. He generally only has to make the nice and easy throw. But that doesn't mean he never has a tough play to make—a play that requires agility and arm strength.

In this chapter, Jerry Hairston Jr. talks about how to make the routine—and not-so-routine—play at second base.

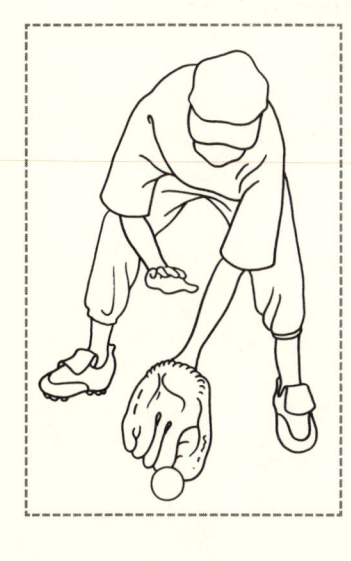

How do you field a routine ground ball?

I think of it as if I'm landing an airplane.

When the ball is approaching you, you want to be slow and controlled on your way down to get the ball, like an airplane when it's about to land. Make sure you keep your eye on the ball, and your head down. You also need to keep your glove out in front of you, flat on the ground.

Why should your glove be flat on the ground?

Because that way, the ball won't go underneath your glove. Plus, if the ball takes a **bad hop,** you can adjust your glove quicker to catch it. It's easier to adjust from down-to-up than it is from up-to-down. And you want to watch the ball the whole way into your glove at all times.

Does your bare hand come into play when fielding a ground ball?

Fielding a ground ball is like an alligator opening and closing its mouth. You have your bare hand as the top of the alligator mouth, and the glove as the bottom of the mouth. Then you want to snap the ball into your glove, just like an alligator would snap its mouth shut.

What's the best throwing position once you've caught the ball?

After you've fielded the ball, you should have your body **squared to the target.** Ideally, you want to hit your target in the chest with your throw. It's just a regular throw: square your feet, face the first baseman, and throw the ball with a nice **follow-through.**

As a second baseman, you're not very far from first base. So do you make a nice, soft throw?

You should neither baby the throw nor **lob** one over. From second base, it's one of the easiest throws. But in a way, it can be the hardest too, because you're so close that you need to figure out exactly how hard you should throw the ball. That's not always so easy.

Make sure you concentrate on every play, but also stay relaxed. You never want to be lazy with your throws. Once you've done it properly, and you've done it often enough, throws to first should become routine.

How do you make a play on a ball to your right side?

It depends how far the ball is to my right. If it's only a little to my right and it's kind of out of my reach, I'll go to the **backhand** to make the play. But if you can get in front of the ball, you should. You want to get in front of the ball as much as you can.

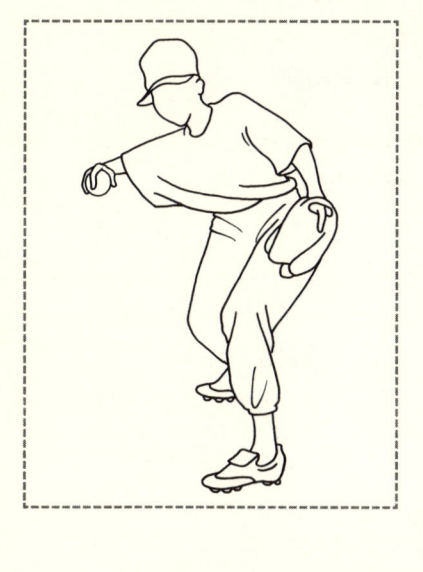

How do you make a throw once you have backhanded a ball?

The most important thing is to make sure you catch the ball first. Then you want to get yourself in a ready-to-throw position, setting your feet as quickly as possible. I like to throw on the run sometimes. But if it's a routine backhand play, set your feet first, look where you're throwing, and then let it fly.

There's a runner on first base and one or no outs. A ground ball is hit to your left. What do you do?

On a play like that, I want to get the **force** at second, but it can be difficult sometimes. Go where the ball takes you. If the ball is behind you a little when you catch it on your left-hand side, then you should make a controlled spin toward right field. You'll wind up facing second base and you can make your throw.

If the ball is in front of you and slightly to your left, you have an opportunity to get in front of it. Once you grab the ball, do a little spin toward the pitcher's mound to face second base. Then throw to second for the out. But whatever you do, fix your eyes on your target and set your feet before you throw.

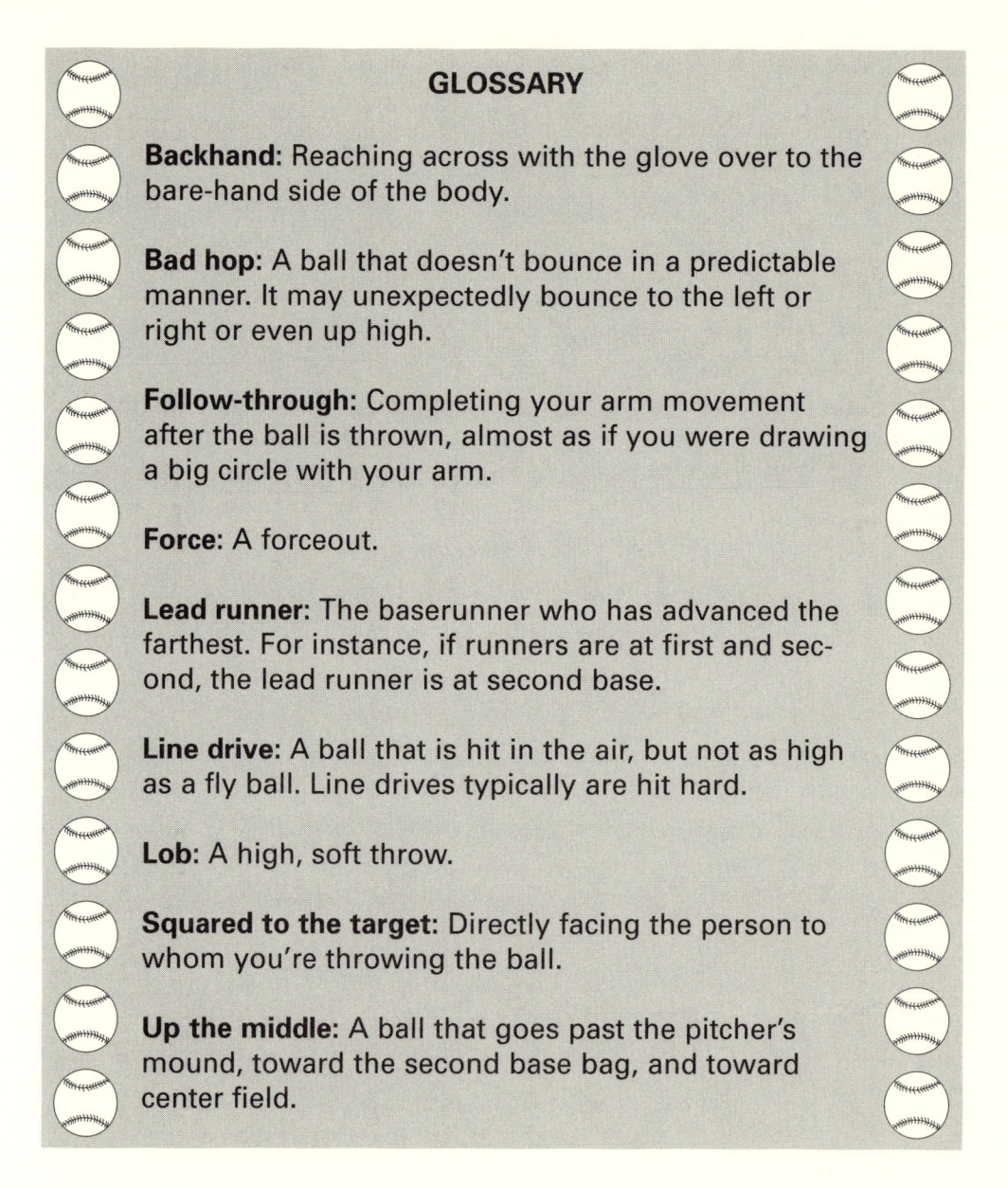

GLOSSARY

Backhand: Reaching across with the glove over to the bare-hand side of the body.

Bad hop: A ball that doesn't bounce in a predictable manner. It may unexpectedly bounce to the left or right or even up high.

Follow-through: Completing your arm movement after the ball is thrown, almost as if you were drawing a big circle with your arm.

Force: A forceout.

Lead runner: The baserunner who has advanced the farthest. For instance, if runners are at first and second, the lead runner is at second base.

Line drive: A ball that is hit in the air, but not as high as a fly ball. Line drives typically are hit hard.

Lob: A high, soft throw.

Squared to the target: Directly facing the person to whom you're throwing the ball.

Up the middle: A ball that goes past the pitcher's mound, toward the second base bag, and toward center field.

★★★★★★★★★★★★★★★★★★★★★★★★★★★★★★

EASY AS 1-2-3!

In general, the second baseman tends to be an overlooked player on any team.

He's usually not a power hitter. He might not be as quick in the field, or have as strong an arm, as the shortstop. But he's steady. That's the term most often applied to a second baseman. He's a player who helps the team win without being the big star. But every now and then, a second baseman will have his moment in the sun, too. The Philadelphia Phillies' Mickey Morandini enjoyed his on September 20, 1992.

The Phillies were playing the Pittsburgh Pirates at Pittsburgh's Three Rivers Stadium. The Pirates had Philadelphia pitcher Curt Schilling in a jam in the bottom of the sixth inning, with the game tied at 1–1. Andy Van Slyke was on second base and Barry Bonds was on first. Jeff King was the batter.

Schilling threw a pitch, and King hit a **line drive** that appeared headed **up the middle** for a base hit. Van Slyke took off from second, hoping to score. Bonds was also on the move.

But Morandini ran a few steps and caught the ball in the air for an out. Then he quickly stepped on the second-base bag, doubling up Van Slyke for the second out on the play. When he saw Bonds coming his way, the alert Morandini ran him down and tagged him out…completing the rare unassisted triple play.

In a matter of seconds, Morandini had gone from being just another very good, steady second baseman to the brightest star on the baseball diamond. But unfortunately for the Phillies, Morandini's brilliance didn't spark them to a win. Pittsburgh ultimately won the game, 3–2.

HERE'S THE SITUATION

You're playing second base. Your team is ahead by three runs in the middle innings and there's a runner at first base, with one out. The batter hits a soft, high-bouncing ball a little to your left. You take a few steps to your left and you field the ball cleanly.

Should you spin around and throw to second base to get the **lead runner** out? Or should you just be content with getting the out at first?

HERE'S THE SOLUTION

Make the play to first. It should be a short, simple throw, and you'll probably have plenty of time to get the runner.

Throwing to second could be risky. Yes, you always want to throw out the lead runner whenever you can, but you also want to play smart. You're ahead by three runs, so why take the chance?

If you try to spin around and make the throw to second, the runner could beat the throw. Then the opposition would have two runners on, and only one out. And you'd be in a jam, because the tying run is coming to the plate. So get the easy out. Leave the other team with one runner on at second base, but only one out left in the inning.

★★★★★ MEMORIES ★★★★★

I remember my first at-bat. I was only 8 years old. But before that, I remember crying because my dad, Jerry Hairston Sr., wouldn't put me on a team. He was also a baseball player and he wanted to make sure that I really wanted to play. He didn't want me playing just because of him.

I hit a grand slam on my first at-bat. But it was one of those cheap grand slams…a line drive over the shortstop's head and the ball just kept rolling for days. It's probably still rolling right now. But hey, it was a grand slam!

I played for the Phillies in a league in Naperville, Illinois. I was the shortstop and I played a little center field, too. I used a Black Magic Easton aluminum bat. We had a great team. We were undefeated as an 8- to 9-year-old team. We played every day. It was a great neighborhood of kids.

People knew who my father was, but I just went out and played and had fun. A lot of people thought it was a big deal, having a father who was in the big leagues. But I didn't, since I had been around the game so much already.

We always went to a pizza place or for hot dogs after a game. As long as we played hard, it didn't matter if we won or lost. We just did our best and had fun.

SHORTSTOP

DEREK JETER

The shortstop has to have good range, which is the ability to cover a major part of the infield. He also has to field balls that are hit right at him. Being a successful shortstop begins with good body position, whether **charging the ball,** fielding it in the **shortstop's hole,** or moving to the left for a hard-hit grounder.

In this chapter, All-Star and World Series MVP Derek Jeter offers his suggestions on how to play shortstop.

What's the best body position for fielding a ground ball?

Your legs should be spread apart, maybe shoulder width or a little bit more. You want to make sure your knees are bent. But above all, you have to be comfortable.

Are you standing flat-footed when the ball is coming to you?

No, you want to be on the balls of your feet.

Why on the balls of your feet?

That's the proper stance for any sport. For instance, if you're playing defense in basketball, you have to be on the balls of your feet. Otherwise, you can't move side to side like you need to. If you're flat-footed, someone will make a move and just go right around you. It's the same thing when you're playing baseball. To field ground balls, you have to be able to move from side to side.

What do you do when a ground ball is hit right at you?

First of all, you have to judge how hard the ball is hit. That will tell you if you need to charge the ball. Make sure to **read the hops** to see if you should back up a little to field the ball. But, if possible, you want your momentum moving toward first base as you catch the ground ball. That will put you in good position to throw.

What are you looking at when a ground ball is hit to you?

When you're fielding the ball, your eyes are on the ball. You have to watch it all the way into your glove. A lot of times you'll look at the ball and think you have it, but then it might take a **bad hop** at the last second and you won't be able to catch it cleanly. So you have to make sure you watch it all the way.

What do you do with your bare hand when you're catching a ground ball?

You're not going to catch the ball with your bare hand, but it's good to have it next to the glove as support. You want the bare hand as close to the glove as possible, because that way you can get the ball out of the glove a lot quicker to make the throw.

Once you've fielded the ball, how do you throw to first base?

When you're throwing to first, make sure your momentum is going toward the bag. Your body shouldn't go in one direction while you're trying to throw in another. You also want your feet firmly planted underneath you, so your whole body is under control.

It's not necessary to point your left shoulder to where you're throwing, but you should always try to be moving in the direction you're throwing.

What do you do on a ground ball to your left?

It depends on how hard it's hit. You have to decide if you can get in front of it, or if you have to play it with one hand. There are a lot of things that come into play when you're making these decisions. Are you playing on grass or turf? How fast is the runner? Was it a right-handed hitter or a left-handed hitter?

What about a ball to your right?

That's probably the hardest play, if you have to catch the ball on your **backhand.** In that situation, you're running away from first base when you field the ball. So when you do get the ball, you have to quickly redirect your momentum to first to make the throw. That's the toughest thing to do. And it's also the longest throw.

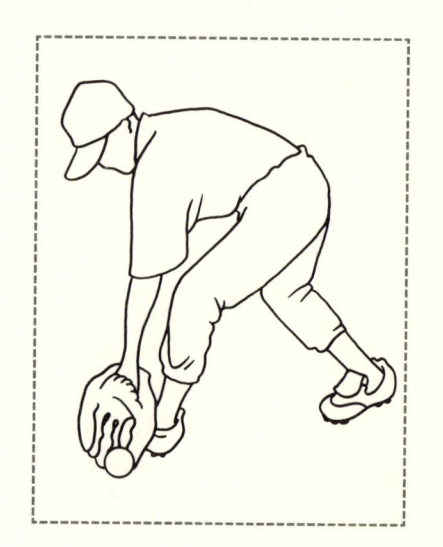

You have to gather yourself and get your body under control, if you can. Sometimes you might have to throw off-balance, though. It all depends on how much time you have.

How do you make a backhand pickup?

Ideally, you'd like to get the ball going to the middle of your left foot. That way, you

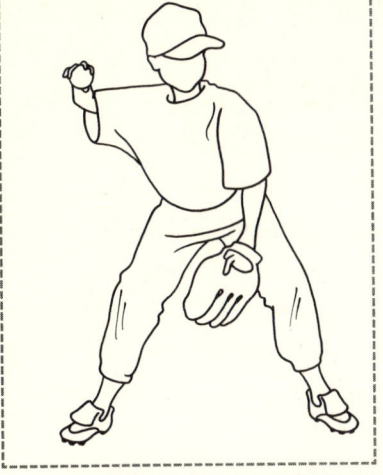

don't have to really reach for the ball. But sometimes, if the ball is hit hard, you don't have a choice and you have to get it any way you can.

How do you make a throw from the shortstop hole?

You have to make sure you **plant** yourself. Get the ball, stop, gather yourself, and then throw. You put your right foot down, push off that foot, and throw.

GLOSSARY

Backhand: Reaching across with the glove over to the bare-hand side of the body.

Bad hop: A ball that doesn't bounce in a predictable manner. It may unexpectedly bounce to the left or right or even up high.

Charge the ball: Move forward toward the ball, rather than stay in your position and wait for it to come to you.

Shortstop hole: The space on the infield dirt between the third baseman and the shortstop.

Plant: Press your back foot into the ground so you can push off that foot to make a stronger throw.

Read the hops: Watch the ball carefully, so you can judge where the bounces will take it.

A PEBBLE ROCKS THE YANKEES!

When the ball left Bill Virdon's bat, it appeared as if the Pittsburgh Pirates outfielder had hit into a double play that would leave the New York Yankees only four outs shy of another World Championship.

But there was no double play. The ball hit a pebble in the dirt at shortstop, which caused it to take an unexpected hop up, striking Yankees' shortstop, Tony Kubek, in the throat.

Kubek fell to the ground in pain as the ball bounced away. Virdon was safe at first, and the lead runner was safe at second on the bad-hop single. So instead of having two outs and no one on base, the Pirates now had two men on and no outs. And they took advantage of the big break by scoring five runs in the inning for a 9–7 lead.

The Yankees rallied to tie the game at 9–9 in the top of the ninth inning, but all that did was set up second baseman Bill Mazeroski to become the toast of Pittsburgh and the baseball world. Mazeroski slugged a home run in the bottom of the ninth, giving the Pirates a 10–9 win and the 1960 World Championship. But while it was Mazeroski's home run that eventually won Pittsburgh the World Series title, it was a tiny pebble that really helped the Pirates rock the Yankees.

HERE'S THE SITUATION

There's a runner at third base, with one out, in the last inning. You're playing shortstop, and your team is ahead by four runs. You're playing back at your normal position. The batter hits a hard ground ball to you. The runner from third breaks for home. You know he doesn't have great speed, and the ball is hit pretty hard to you. You field the ball cleanly.

Where should you throw?

Home?

Or first?

HERE'S THE SOLUTION

Get the easier out: throw to first base.

You might be able to throw the runner out at home, but it's a tougher play because it's not a forceout. The catcher will have to grab the ball and apply a tag before the runner hits home plate. There's too much risk in this type of play—the ball could be knocked out of the glove by a sliding runner, the catcher could miss the ball, or your throw might be off-line.

It's not worth the risk. If the runner does score, you're still up three runs, and once you get the runner out at first base, you'll have two outs in the last inning.

★★★★★ MEMORIES ★★★★★

I just remember the whole Little League thing…being out there trying to act like everyone I'd see on TV, pretending I was a big league player. I was a Yankee fan, so I pretended to be all of the Yankees at some point.

We moved around a lot when I was a kid. I played in the Westwood Little League, the Oakwood league, and the Eastwood league. They were all in Michigan.

You always have to have a good time. If you have fun and practice every chance you get, you're going to be successful.

THIRD BASE

SCOTT BROSIUS

There are times when a third baseman doesn't need a glove to make a play. He can just use his bare hand. But fielding a slow roller or a bunt that way can be tough, especially if you're on the run.

In this chapter, World Series MVP Scott Brosius reveals how to make this difficult play, as well as tips on other aspects of playing third base.

What's the best way to pick up the ball with your bare hand on a slow roller or a bunt?

There are two ways guys are taught to catch with a bare hand. The first is to run over and kind of pluck the ball from the top with your hand. The other way is to come up behind the ball and scoop it up. I've always thought that scooping the ball was best, so that's what I do.

Why do you prefer the "scooping" method?

Well, when you're fielding ground balls in practice, it's always better to keep your body and hands low. That makes it easier to react with your hands and catch a bad hop quicker. For the bare hand play, I like the idea of having my hand down, really close to the ground. That way, if the ball stays on the ground, I'm there to catch it. And if the ball should come up, then I can move my hand up to meet it.

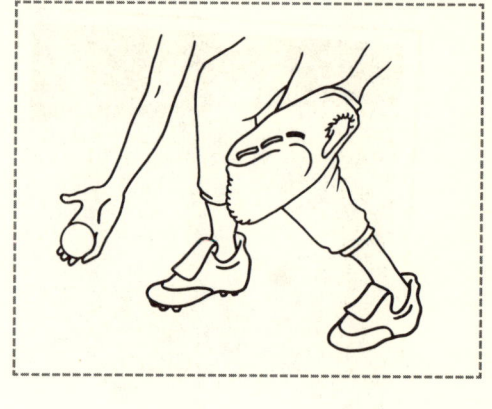

Once you've fielded the ball with your bare hand, do you set your feet the same way as you would on a routine ground ball?

When you're taking a slow roller, you never really **plant** your feet. You're going to have to make your throw on the run. That's just the nature of the play.

What's your body position when you're making this type of play?

On a slow roller, I want to get my body to the right side of the ball. That way, I'm coming straight in on the ball, and I'm not running away from first base. Also, when I'm throwing the ball, my body is going directly toward home plate instead of falling into foul territory. If I fall into foul territory, then I'm throwing away from my body and the throw might not be as accurate. That's why I want to come straight in on the ball.

How do you throw the ball?

Generally, you're taught to keep your wrist above the ball when you throw. So even if you're throwing from a low body position, you want

the ball in your bare hand to be above your glove hand when you let it go, not pointing straight down. That way, the throw won't **sink** on its way to first base.

Once you've fielded the ball on a routine grounder, then what do you do?

After you catch the ball, it's important to take a good **crow hop.** The crow hop is like a little rhythm step that helps you get set to throw.

Are you standing still as you field the ball?

It's important to be on your toes after catching the ball, instead of being flat-footed. You'll still have your body's momentum heading to first, which is where you're going to throw. The momentum helps you put more force behind your throw. It also gets you closer to first base so the throw isn't as far.

Generally, your **arm angle** should be up over your shoulder when you make your throw.

GLOSSARY

Arm angle: The position of your arm as you throw the ball.

Crow hop: A short, three-part move—similar to a dance step—players use to get their feet in a good position to make a strong throw.

Plant: Press your feet into the ground.

Sink: Drop toward the ground. The ball dips suddenly as it reaches the target.

TRIPLE THE FUN, TWICE!

Triple plays don't happen very often. But on July 17, 1990, at Fenway Park, the Boston Red Sox grounded into a triple play. Not once...but twice in the same game! And both times, it was Minnesota's Gary Gaetti, Al Newman, and Kent Hrbek who tripled the Twins' fun and snuffed out any possible Red Sox rallies.

In the fourth inning, the bases were loaded. The Red Sox had put Minnesota pitcher Scott Erickson in deep trouble. But on Erickson's next pitch, Tom Brunansky hit a hard grounder to Gaetti, the Twins' third baseman. Gaetti caught the ball, right near the third-base bag. He calmly stepped on the base. One out. Then he threw to Newman, covering second base, and Newman stepped on that bag. Two outs. Newman quickly relayed the ball to Hrbek, Minnesota's first baseman. The throw beat Brunansky. Three outs...a triple play! There were high fives all around as the Twins raced to their dugout.

In the eighth inning, there was a virtual instant replay. This time, there were runners on first and second base, and up stepped the Red Sox' Jody Reed to the plate. Reed hit the ball on the ground, right at Gaetti. The third baseman stepped on the bag, and threw to Newman at second. Newman relayed the ball to Hrbek. Once again, the Twins had pulled off a triple play!

It was the first time in Major League history that one team had turned two triple plays in the same game. The Red Sox, however, had the last laugh. Boston won the game, 1–0.

HERE'S THE SITUATION

It's the last inning. You're up by one run. There's one out and the opposing team has runners at first and third. You're playing third base and the batter hits a hard one-hopper right at you. The runner from third breaks for home as soon as the ball is hit.

Do you throw home in an attempt to cut down the tying run at the plate? Or should you try for a double play, which could end the game and give your team the victory?

HERE'S THE SOLUTION

There's really no easy answer here. You need to figure out what to do as the ball is approaching you. A lot of information must be processed quickly.

Is the ball hit straight at you?

How fast a runner is the batter?

If the answers to those questions are "Yes, the ball is coming right to me," and "No, the batter doesn't run well," then you may want to take a chance on turning the game-ending double play.

But if the ball isn't hit to you that hard or if the batter is pretty fast, your odds of turning the double play are slim. In this case, you might want to throw home to stop the tying run from scoring.

No matter what, you want to make sure you get at least one out on the play, whether it's at home, second, or even at first base.

★ ★ ★ ★ ★ **MEMORIES** ★ ★ ★ ★ ★

The thing that stands out for me the most is how much fun the game was. When I was 9 years old, I didn't understand the difference between a hit and an error. I didn't know what an RBI was. I just played baseball. And if I got on second base, I figured I'd just hit a double, no matter how I got there. I didn't know any better.

I think the key for that age, especially about 9 or 10 years old, is that the game is supposed to be fun. You're not trying to make it to the big leagues as a 9-year-old. You're supposed to play because you enjoy it. Go out there and have fun. Don't worry about how many hits you're getting. As you get older and have been playing a little longer, then you can start worrying about wins and losses.

I played in the Evergreen Little League in Vancouver, Washington. I pitched and played shortstop. I was nothing out of the ordinary. I was a small kid, just like anybody else out there.

I'd put my uniform on 5 hours before the game. I just couldn't wait to get out there and play. The sponsor for my teams when I was 10 to 12 years old was A&W Root Beer. But we never got as much root beer as I thought we should!

ROBERTO ALOMAR

NOMAR GARCIAPARRA

THE DOUBLE PLAY
(PART 1)

THE 6-4-3 DOUBLE PLAY

(Shortstop to Second Baseman to First Baseman)

I t's called "The Pitcher's Best Friend." Or the "Twin Killing." But no matter what its nickname, there's nothing that helps a pitcher get out of a jam faster than the Double Play. It requires quick, efficient teamwork performed with ballet-like precision, resulting in two outs on one ground ball.

In this chapter, All-Star shortstop Nomar Garciaparra and All-Star second baseman Roberto Alomar talk about how to "Turn Two." They discuss the responsibilities of both positions and the techniques they use in turning the 6–4–3 and 4–6–3 double plays.

Nomar Garciaparra— The Shortstop's Responsibilities

What is the first thing the shortstop has to do to start a double play?

Rule number one is to catch the ball. Don't worry about anything else until you have the ball in hand. If you're thinking about the runner or the throw you have to make, you might not even catch the ground ball.

What's the best way to catch the ball?

If there's a man on first base, you might be playing closer to the infield grass than you do in your normal position. You might also be a couple of steps closer to second base. But you have to be in the correct fielding position so that, when the ground ball comes to you, you can field it cleanly with two hands.

Once you've fielded the ball cleanly, what kind of throw do you make to the second baseman to start the double play?

It depends where the ball is hit.

If the ball is hit right at you or to your left, then field it and give a firm underhand toss to the second baseman. Try to hit him in the chest with the toss. Throw it underhand so he can see the ball the whole way. For this type of throw, the ball

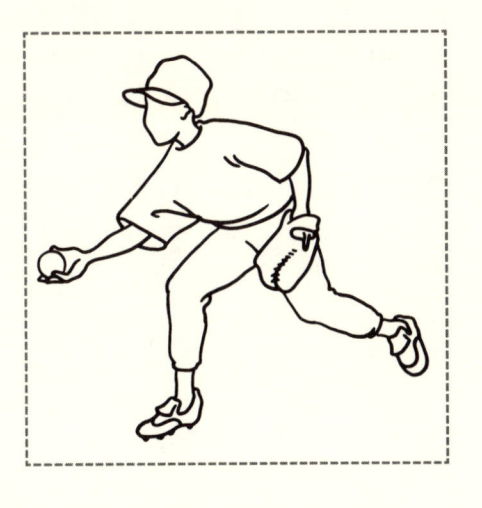

is in your bare hand and your glove is out of the way. That makes it easier for the second baseman to see the ball.

What if the ball is hit to your right?

If the ball is hit to your right, it's just like any other ground ball. Get in front of it and get yourself in a good fielding position. As always, field the ball with two hands.

Because you're trying to turn a double play, your left foot should be slightly back when you're ready to field the ball. That way, because your right foot is a bit in front of your left, your body will be a bit open, almost turned toward second base. So as you field the ball, your body will already be in position to throw the ball to second.

Do you make the same kind of underhand throw to second base if you field the ball to your right?

No. From this position, I make an **overhand** throw, nice and firm. This gives the second baseman a throw that's easy to handle. It's a nice quick motion on this throw. You're not winding up. You throw it like a dart.

What is your body position when you make this throw?

Stay low. You don't want to stand up to make the throw, because that takes time. You're already down low in the fielding position, so stay in that position.

What if you can't field the ball in a perfect position?

If a ball is hit to your right, you have to get the ball and pivot your left foot a bit as you field the ball. Open up your body toward second base so that you will be in a good throwing position. You don't want to have to throw **sidearm** across your body, because it's harder to control that type of throw. Face your chest toward the target to make a more accurate throw.

Where are you aiming when you make your throw to second base?

The throw should be right where the second baseman wants it.

Some second basemen like the throw to be a little behind the bag, but some want it right over the bag. You have to work with your second baseman and practice this, so you'll know where he wants the ball.

Roberto Alomar—
The Second Baseman's Responsibilities

What's the first thing a second baseman does to turn a double play when the ground ball is hit to the shortstop?

You get to the bag as early as you can, just in case there's a bad throw. You'll have more time to react that way.

When the shortstop throws the ball, where do you place your feet so you can make the pivot and then throw the ball to first base?

The best idea is to place your left foot on top of the bag and wait for the throw. As you catch the ball, lean toward third base. Your right foot should be in front of your left so that it's pointed toward the third-base bag. Then you can push off the bag with your left foot when you throw.

Where are your hands when the shortstop throws you the ball?

Your hands are out toward the shortstop, ready to catch the ball. Always use two hands to catch the ball. I try to catch the ball so it's on the right side of my chest.

Why do you want to catch the ball on the right side of your chest?

That way I'm ready to catch the ball and throw it, almost at the same time. My body will be balanced and under control, which helps me make a more accurate throw. If I catch the ball on my left side, I have to bring the ball back over to my right side in order to throw. That takes time, which allows the runner extra steps, making it tougher to turn the double play.

How important is it to have "quick hands"?

Nobody has quick hands. To me, quick feet make quick hands. If you can move your feet quickly around the bag, your hands will move quicker at the same time. If you have slow feet, your hands are going to be slow, too.

Are there different ways to turn a double play?

One way you can do it, as I mentioned earlier, is to move across the bag, toward third base as you catch the ball. Another way is to "hide" from the runner. You catch the ball, push off the back of the bag with your left foot, and throw to first. That way, the base is between you and the sliding runner, so he can't slide into you.

How difficult is turning a double play for a second baseman?

It's the toughest thing for a second baseman to do!

Why?

Because you don't know where the runner is when you're making the play. As a shortstop turning a double play, the play is in front of you. You can see the runner. But a second baseman has his body turned away from the runner, so he can't see the action.

THE DOUBLE PLAY
(PART 2)

THE 4-6-3
DOUBLE PLAY

(Second baseman to shortstop to first baseman)

Roberto Alomar—
The Second Baseman's Responsibilities

What's the first thing a second baseman has to do to start a double play?

The first thing you have to do is catch the ball. You can't make the throw without having the ball in hand first.

How do you field the ball?

I try to field the ball in front of me, to reach for the ball. I don't want the ball to get too close to my body. I want to reach out and catch it in front of me.

Do you catch the ball with one hand or two hands?

Two hands, in case you get a bad hop. If you do get a bad hop, you've got a chance to block it with either hand and still get at least one out on the play. Also, you should catch the ball with two hands so that you can quickly transfer the ball from your glove to your throwing hand.

What's your body position when you field the ball?

Your body is down low when you're fielding. Your butt has to be down, your knees are bent, and your head is down so you can see the ball better…especially if it's a bad bounce. If your butt and upper body stay up, you might not see the ball and you'll get **handcuffed.** If you get a bad hop in that position, you can't do anything about it. You can't react quickly enough.

When you catch the ball, is your body turned toward second base to be in position to make the throw?

No. You should catch the ball first, and then angle your body. That's a problem for some big league second basemen. They try to turn before they catch the ball. If you do that and get a bad hop, you're going to miss the ball.

Where do you position yourself in a double-play situation?

My father, Sandy Alomar Sr., who played many years in the big leagues as an infielder, always taught me to play to my weaknesses. The toughest play for a second baseman is the backhand play, which is a ground ball to his right. The easiest play for a second baseman is a ball hit right at him or a ball to his left. So, if you position yourself a little more to your right, there will be less backhand territory to cover and the play **up the middle** can be made more easily.

What type of throw do you make to the shortstop?

There are two types of throws. If I field the ball where I'm standing or to my right, I'll flip it either backhand or underhand. But if I catch the ball to my left, I throw overhand.

How do your feet move when you throw the ball?

There are different ways to move your feet.

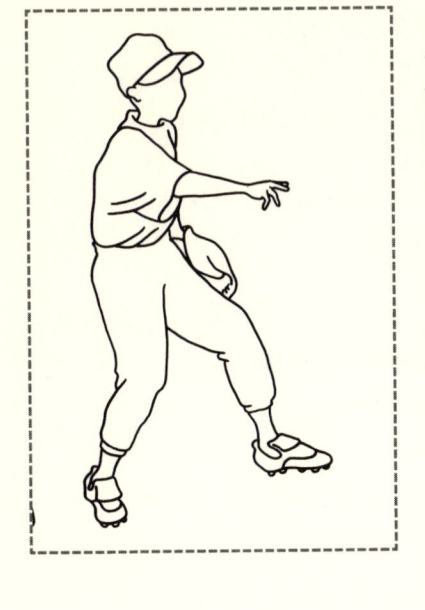

If the ball is hit straight at you, you can twist your toes and feet toward the second base bag after you catch it and throw or flip the ball. If you're going to flip the ball, you catch it and turn toward second base.

If I catch the ball to my left, I'll turn toward first base and then around to face second. That gives me more momentum and I'll be able to make a stronger throw. If you turn the other way, you'll wind up throwing the ball lower with your arm and the ball will sink. That's a tougher throw for the shortstop to handle. Whenever you throw, though, you want to be squared up with your shoulders facing the shortstop.

Where do you aim your throw?

I throw the ball to the outside of the bag, to the left of the short-stop. But it depends where the shortstop likes to catch the ball to turn a double play. I played with Cal Ripken Jr., and he liked his throw right over the middle of the bag. I've also played with Omar Vizquel, and he liked it on the outside of the bag.

The Shortstop's Responsibilities—
Nomar Garciaparra

Where do you go when the second baseman is fielding the ball?

Get behind the bag. You're not standing on the bag. You're actually angled with the second baseman, so the base is in a straight line between you and the second baseman. Always have your chest facing him. That way, no matter where he throws the ball, you'll be in a good athletic position to catch the ball.

Are you just standing still behind the bag waiting for the throw?

No. I suggest taking short, choppy steps because you don't want to get too far ahead of yourself. You can still maneuver left or right, but you'll have some momentum this way.

What do you do when the ball is thrown to you?

When you see the ball coming, keep both hands close to each other and try to receive the ball at your chest. Try not to hold your arms straight out. Keep them close to your body. The closer your hands are together, the easier it is for the exchange of the ball from the glove to the throwing hand. This way, you're right in your throwing motion as you're catching the ball.

Why don't you reach out for the ball?

If your arms are extended from your body, you still have to catch the ball, bring it in, and then throw. So the closer everything is to your body, the quicker you'll be in the set position to make a throw.

Then what?

After you catch the ball, you force your body back into a good throwing position. Turn your left shoulder to face your target and make your throw.

How do you tag the bag?

You drag your right foot across the back of the bag as you're catching the ball. It's kind of a slide across the back of the bag. You don't step on top of the bag. You're throwing and touching the bag at the same time, all in one motion.

Are your eyes on the runner or on the target at first base?

Your eyes are on the ball. Once you receive the ball, you can shift your attention to the target at first base. You can't be too concerned with the runners. If you're in correct position, you throw the ball. Then you either prepare to jump so the runner doesn't hit you with his slide, or you clear yourself out of the way, moving toward right field after throwing the ball.

GLOSSARY

Handcuffed: An infielder prefers to field a grounder with his hands out in front of him. But if a ground ball takes a bad hop and it's impossible to field it with your hands out in front, it has to be fielded with the hands close to the body. That makes it a difficult play, and the player is referred to as being handcuffed.

Overhand: The usual throwing motion in which the arm moves up and over, palm down and fingers facing the target when releasing the baseball.

Sidearm: A throwing motion in which the arm is about waist-high and parallel to the ground when releasing the ball.

Up the middle: A ball that goes past the pitcher's mound, out toward the second base bag, and toward center field.

★ ★

YER OUT!

The Boston Red Sox' Dwight Evans was perched at third base, and Rich Gedman was at first base, after grounding a single to right field. There was one out in the top of the fifth inning, and the Sox were trailing the Oakland Athletics, 6–5, in Game 3 of the 1988 American League Championship Series. Oakland already had a 2–0 lead in the best-of-seven series, so the Red Sox were getting desperate, trying to scratch for every run they could.

Gene Nelson was pitching for Oakland. The next Red Sox batter was Jody Reed, who hit a bouncer to the third baseman, Carney Lansford. His throw to second was in plenty of time to get Gedman for the second out of the inning.

Gedman slid hard into the second baseman, Mike Gallego, so Reed was safe at first. Evans scored what appeared to be the tying run. But the second base umpire Ken Kaiser ruled that Gedman had gone out of the baseline in his slide, which is a violation of the rules. As a result, Reed was also called out on the play. The Red Sox vehemently protested the umpire's call, but to no avail.

Gedman and Reed were called out on the double play, so Evans's run didn't count. The Athletics maintained their 6–5 lead. And Boston never caught up. The Red Sox lost the game, 10–6. They lost the next day, too, as Oakland swept the series and earned a berth in the World Series.

HERE'S THE SITUATION

It's the bottom of the last inning. There are runners at first and third with only one out, and you have a 4–3 lead. A ground ball is hit to you at shortstop.

Should you try to turn a double play, even though the tying run will score if you fail? Or should you field the ball, check the runner at third to see what he's doing, and then make your decision?

HERE'S THE SOLUTION

What should you do? Well, it depends.

There are a lot of little facts you need to know in making this decision. How fast is the runner? How hard was the ball hit? Where was the ball hit? Is it an easy double-play ball? How good is the second baseman at turning a double play?

Whatever you do, you have to make a decision fast. In this situation, there isn't one correct answer. All you can do is try to make the best decision, and do so as quickly as possible!

★★★★★ MEMORIES ★★★★★

NOMAR GARCIAPARRA

I remember the first time I put on a glove, and the first time I actually played Little League tee-ball.

In my first practice, I was at first base. Some of the parents were coaches. One of the coaches threw a ball at me, and she threw it pretty hard. It didn't come close to hitting my glove. It hit me smack in the nose, and I started bleeding. It absolutely crushed me. I was only 5 years old. But I never missed another ball again.

Even in my first year of tee-ball, "No-Nonsense" was my nickname. I never fooled around, not even at 5 years old. Kids were throwing their gloves around, joking around. But I always took the game seriously. I was always focused. I still enjoyed playing, but I never fooled around. I'd get mad if the other guys fooled around.

One time when I was older, I didn't know what inning we were in. I thought it was the last inning. I remember coming up to the plate, making an out and thinking the game was over. I threw my helmet against the fence, and I kicked my bat because I was so upset. I thought I had lost the game. But there really was one more inning.

My dad was the coach. "You're sitting down," he said. "I never want to see you fired up like that again." That lesson taught me that you have to deal with failure as much as you do with success. It also taught me to pay attention to the inning. I never threw my helmet in that league again.

There were some successful moments, too. I remember being in a league championship game when I was 12, and my cousin was on the team. We were losing by two runs in our last at-bat. My cousin ending up walking, and I hit a home run that tied the game. It was just a huge moment. It was a championship game, and there were a lot of people in the stands. I couldn't believe it. I remember coming in and seeing the smile on my dad's face. He was coaching. He was like, "Wow, I can't believe you did that."

We scored a run in the next inning and we won the championship.

—*Nomar Garciaparra*

ROBERTO ALOMAR

I remember learning that you always have to practice and play hard—even in the big leagues. That's important for kids to know. I was playing for Toronto and we were facing Oakland in the playoffs. My dad was there. He had played a long time in the big leagues as an infielder. I took pregame infield practice like I really didn't want to be out there. My dad took me aside and told me not to bother taking practice if I was going to do it that way. He said to be a professional and take it as hard as if I was playing in a game. I knew that he was right. You always have to take practice hard and do things the right way.

PART 4

OUTFIELD

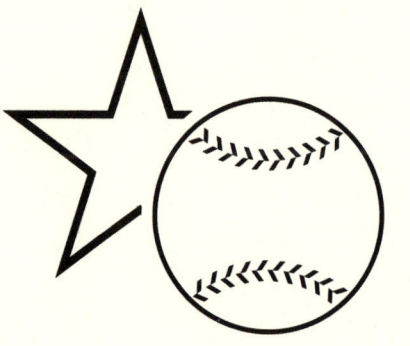

CATCHING FLY BALLS

MATT LAWTON

Standing all the way in the outfield, it may seem like you're far away from the action. And many innings can go by without you being involved in a play. But you can't let your mind wander. You have to be ready for action at all times. When a ball is hit in the air toward you, you have to track it down.

In this chapter, All-Star Matt Lawton discusses a few basics of outfield play.

What are you thinking while you're standing in the outfield?

At the big-league level, you always need to be in position to make the next play. You're thinking about where your next throw is going to be so you can position yourself to make it. For instance, if you're going to throw to second base, you want to have your weight behind you. Your body should be set and balanced before you take all your momentum toward second and throw to the base.

When you're in the outfield, you're watching the pitch to see where the ball will go. You also want to think about the tendencies of the hitters—do they pull the ball or do they hit to the opposite field? That will help you figure out where they might hit the ball so you can better position yourself.

Do you look at the hitter when the pitch is being thrown?

Sure. This will help you get tips on where he might hit the ball. For instance, let's say a right-handed hitter was late with an earlier swing and fouled the ball off to right field. If you're playing right field, then you might move a step or two closer to the right-field foul line. There's a good chance he might hit the ball in that direction again.

What's the "ready" position for an outfielder?

I consider the ready position to be having your feet shoulder-width apart, being bent at the knees, and staying on the balls of your feet. That way, you're ready to go wherever the ball is hit. You can either break in on the ball or break back on the ball. You should always watch the ball off the bat.

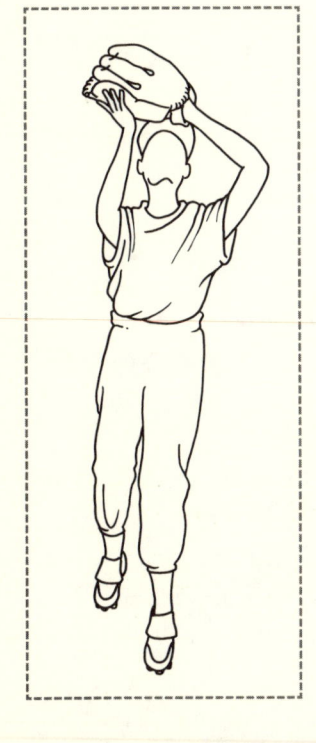

When a routine fly ball is hit right at you, how do you catch the ball?

When I have the chance, I like to catch the ball almost directly above my cap, with both of my eyes on the ball. Sometimes you won't be able to do this. You might have to dive for a ball or reach for it after a long run. But you always want to watch the ball into your glove.

If the ball is above you, your eyes are on the ball at all times. If the wind shifts the ball in a certain direction, you can still keep your eyes on it. But if the ball drops down below your eyes, the wind may catch it and you could lose track of the ball for a split second.

110

Do you catch the ball with one hand or two?

I catch the ball with one hand. I feel I have more reach to the ball that way. But you should always catch the ball in the way you feel most comfortable.

Isn't it important to have your bare hand close to the glove when you make a catch?

Yes. Even though I catch with my glove hand, my bare hand is ready, so I can make a quick **transfer** of the ball from my glove to my hand.

What's the best way to run after a fly ball?

You have to stay on the balls of your feet, instead of on your heels. If you run on your heels, it looks as if the ball is bouncing in the air. Of course, the ball's not actually bouncing...your head is! So if you run on the balls of your feet and keep your head as still as possible, it will be easier to track down the ball.

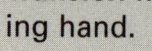
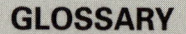 **GLOSSARY**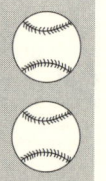

Transfer: Moving the ball from the glove to the throwing hand.

THAT'S USING HIS HEAD!

On May 26, 1993, Jose Canseco gave Cleveland's Carlos Martinez a home run by using his head. Literally.

In the fourth inning of the game, Martinez hit a long fly ball that sailed toward the fence in right-center field. Canseco, playing right field for the Texas Rangers, drifted back on the ball. His body was angled with his right shoulder closest to the wall. As he reached the warning track, Canseco reached up with his glove hand. But the ball didn't go in his glove. In fact, it didn't even touch his glove. Canseco had missed the ball—completely. The ball hit the top of Canseco's head—and plopped over the fence for a home run!

HERE'S THE SITUATION

There are runners at first and second. It's the last inning. There is one out and your team is ahead by two runs. You're playing right field. The batter hits a fly ball toward right-center. You take off after the ball, but quickly realize it will not be an easy, routine catch. To have any chance of catching the ball, you're going to have to dive for it.

Should you dive? Or should you play it safe and just give the batter a single?

★★★★★★★★★★★★★★★★★★

HERE'S THE SOLUTION

In this case, it's better to be safe than sorry. Give up a single to the batter. You can even give up a run. You always want to be aggressive. But in this situation, you shouldn't try for a diving catch unless you're absolutely certain you will be able to come up with the ball. Why not? Because, if the ball bounces past you, both runners will probably score and the game will be tied. The batter will get either a double or a triple, putting him in scoring position to win the game.

It's better to play it safe. Let the ball fall in for a base hit. If the runner from second is going home, don't even attempt to throw him out. Instead, throw to third base. If you do throw to home, the runner from first will probably make it to third, with the batter moving up to second base. If that happens, the tying run will be at third base and the go-ahead run will be at second. So play it safe: let the ball bounce, and then throw to third. This will most likely force the player running from first base to stop at second. Then your team is still up a run, and you also have the chance to turn a double play to get out of the jam.

★ ★ ★ ★ ★ **MEMORIES** ★ ★ ★ ★ ★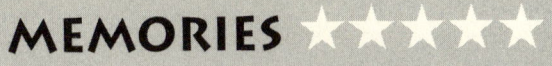

My dad, Matt, was my coach. He was a little hard on me, but he kept me going. I thank him for it all the time because he kept me into baseball.

I grew up in Saucier, Mississippi, which is a really small town. I played in the Little League there. Local stores sponsored us and my team was named the Party Patch. That was the first team I ever played for. I was 9 years old. Instead of outfield, I played shortstop. I remember going out there, and really enjoying the game.

I had lots of favorite players when I was a kid. But I wanted to be just like my dad. He played the game, too. I was batboy when he played on a semi-pro team on Sundays. That was a lot of fun.

In our Little League, we didn't have fences. You would hit the ball as far as you could and just start running. I did hit some homers though. I guess you could call them inside-the-park homers.

Our infield was all dirt. The fields were pretty bad, but I didn't know any better at the time. That was back in the days when we'd play ball in the streets, too, and take ground balls off the concrete, so those fields were no problem!

Matt Lawton

THROWING

BRADY ANDERSON

An outfielder doesn't just catch fly balls. Although that is a major part of the job, he has to throw the ball too. Whether the outfielder throws after catching a fly ball or fielding a base hit, he sometimes has an opportunity to throw out a baserunner. The chance often comes at an important moment in the game. Everything happens quickly, with very little margin for error.

In this chapter, All-Star Brady Anderson talks about the art of throwing out baserunners.

***Before you can throw the ball, you have to catch it first.
Are you standing still when you catch the ball?***

I was always taught to get behind the ball. You should try to come in on the ball to catch it. This will help with your throw too, because as you catch the ball, your momentum is going forward.

Of course, this doesn't always happen. Even in the big leagues, you'll see some guys standing completely still. Sometimes it's hard to judge where the ball will be, so you just have to make the catch. But if you can, you always want to be moving into the ball.

What are you looking at before a pitch is thrown?

I always concentrate on the hitter's **contact area.** But you shouldn't stare at it all of the time…only when the pitch is being thrown. It's best to look around between pitches, maybe at the pitcher or at the runners on base. But when the ball is pitched, always focus on the contact area.

Why don't you want to concentrate on the contact area at all times?

Sometimes if you stare at one place too long, you start to zone out a little bit. You might lose your focus.

What's the best body position as a pitch is thrown?

Whatever position you feel is comfortable. You might want to bend over slightly and take a step forward as the pitch is approaching home plate. Picture a tennis player returning a serve. First, he creeps forward a bit. Then, when he's about to go after the ball, both of his feet are on the ground.

It's the same technique when you're throwing a baseball. You take what I call a "split step" as the pitch is thrown. Take a little hop and land on both feet as the pitch arrives in the hitter's zone. Your weight should be balanced. That way, you're ready to run in the direction the ball is hit.

When there's a runner on base and you see a ball coming toward you on the ground, how do you approach the ball?

It's important to **charge the ball** hard right away.

Why?

If you're charging in hard, you can stop the runners before you even get to the ball. That's key. If they see you charging really hard, they're less likely to try for another base and you might not have to make a quick throw.

Do you keep running as hard as you can when you get to the ball?

Run as hard as you can until you get close to the ball. Then you should slow down a little. Make sure your body is under control and you'll be more successful fielding the ball.

Where is your glove when you get to the ball?

I put my glove low, where I think the ball will be when I get to it.

What kind of footwork is involved in catching the ball and then quickly throwing to a base?

I'm left-handed. So when I charge in, I catch the ball with my right foot forward, take one **crow hop,** and then come up to throw.

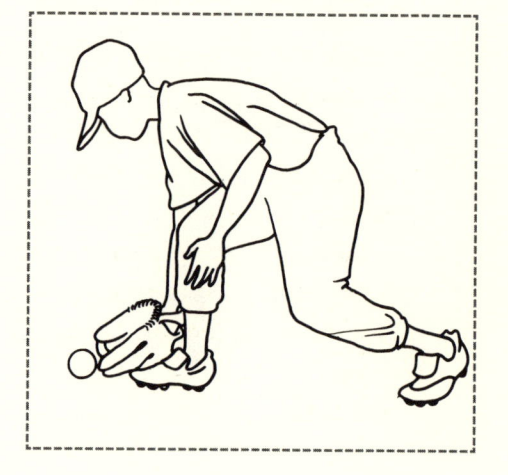

Once you've caught the ball, what's your body position when you make the throw to a base?

You want to keep everything moving toward your **target.** Try not to fall to the side when making the throw. If you position your body to face where you're throwing, you will be more likely to throw straight to the target. But if you fall off to the side, the ball might go off to the side too.

117

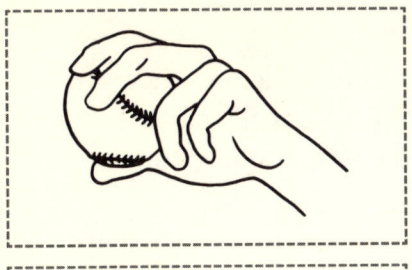

How do you hold the ball to make this type of throw?

It's important to grip the ball with your fingers across the seams. A four-seam throw will keep the ball on a straight line through the air. The throw from the outfield is the longest throw on the field, so the straighter you can make the ball spin, the less chance it will have of **cutting** or **fading** away. Spin is very important.

Is there one **arm angle** *position that's best for this type of throw?*

As an outfielder, it's important to throw from **over the top**. That way, if the ball bounces, it will skip to your target on a straight line.

Where do you aim your throw?

You want to hit the **cutoff man** with your throw. If I'm throwing from center field to third base, I usually aim a little bit above the cutoff man's head. If the throw is a little high, he can always move back a step or two to catch it. But you don't want to throw at his feet and make him play a **short hop.**

GLOSSARY

Arm angle: The position of your arm as you throw the ball.

Charge the ball: Move forward toward the ball rather than stay in your position and wait for it to come to you.

Contact area: The spot where the ball is hit at the plate.

Crow hop: A short, quick three-part move—similar to a dance step—that players use to get their feet in a good position to make a strong throw.

Cutoff man: An infielder who is standing between the outfielder throwing the ball and the infielder catching it. A cutoff man is necessary on a long throw.

Cutting: For a left-handed thrower, a thrown ball that moves quickly from left to right and vice versa.

Fading: For a left-handed thrower, a thrown ball that sails away to the left and vice versa.

Over the top: A throwing motion in which your hand and arm come up parallel to the side of your head upon release of the ball.

Short hop: A bounce that happens close to the fielder. It is just enough out of reach so that he can't catch the ball with his glove before it hits the ground.

Target: Where you want to throw the ball.

HIS CUP RUNNETH OVER!

When the Oakland Athletics' Johnny Damon ripped a ball down the right-field line in a game against the Boston Red Sox on August 8, 2001, it looked like a routine extra-base hit. Maybe it would be a double. Maybe the speedy Damon would even turn it into a triple.

Nothing special. Just your standard extra-base hit, right?

Wrong.

The ball bounced into the right-field corner, hitting the wall in foul territory and then ricocheting back into fair territory. But when Boston right fielder Trot Nixon went to field the ball, hoping to hold Damon to a double or throw him out at third, he suddenly became confused. The ball had disappeared. It had rolled right into a large plastic drinking cup that had fallen onto the field at some point during the inning.

Thinking quickly, Nixon held up his hand, signifying to the umpires that something out of the ordinary had happened. He figured that if he tried to shake the cup and get the ball out, Damon would easily get a triple. Maybe he would even turn the play into an inside-the-park home run. Nixon was hoping that the umpires would call it a ground-rule double, under the same ruling that applies if a ball gets stuck in the padding of a fence.

Meanwhile, Damon circled the bases, touching home plate for what he thought would be a home run. The umpires headed to right field, where Nixon was still standing looking down at the cup, to make a decision. They

★★★★★★★★★★★★★★★★★★★★★★★★★★★★

ruled the play a double for Damon. The Athletics argued, figuring Damon should at least have had third base. But the argument failed.

Once the ruling had been made, Nixon picked up the cup and tried to shake out the ball. But he couldn't. It was wedged in too tightly. So he tossed the cup with the ball still inside it into the stands, giving a lucky fan an unusual souvenir.

Although Damon did not score in the inning, the Athletics eventually won the game, 6–1.

HERE'S THE SITUATION

The game is tied and it's the bottom of the last inning. The opposing team has a runner on second base, and there are two outs. You're playing in the outfield, and it's not as smooth a field as you might find in professional baseball. There are plenty of bumps and divots, which keep the ball from bouncing or rolling in a nice, straight path.

The batter smacks a base hit to you. The ball is hit hard and has a lot of speed as it bounces toward you. The runner from second base is streaking around third base and heading for home, trying to score the winning run. He's a pretty fast runner.

Given the uneven conditions of the field, should you get down on one knee to make sure you at least block the ball? Or should you charge it hard?

HERE'S THE SOLUTION

Charge!

There is no alternative in this situation. You have to put a hard charge on the ball because it's your only chance to throw out the potential winning run at the plate. If you play this one safe, the runner will score easily.

If the ball gets by you or you can't field it cleanly, then that's just the way it goes. The game is over. That happens sometimes. But at least by charging the ball, you gave yourself the best chance to make the tough play.

★★★★★ MEMORIES ★★★★★

I played in the Toluca Lake area of Los Angeles, California, on a team called the Red Sox. I wore number 9, for Hall of Famer Ted Williams. He was my favorite. One year I wore number 6.

My dad was the coach. In fact, he was my coach right up until my junior year in high school. We always won. He was a great coach.

I was pretty advanced when I was young. I don't know how I got to be that way. I didn't have much size. I was a late bloomer. But I was pretty coordinated. Somehow, my dad got me in the league to play when I was 6 years old.

One day, a team was missing a player and I was allowed to play against my dad's team in a practice game. My dad was the umpire. He was coaching, but he was also the umpire for the practice game. I was hitting and he called me out on strikes! I remember the fans were getting all over him, thinking he was showing favoritism to his team because he called me out on strikes. They didn't even know I was his son! Even at 6 years old, I thought that was funny—accusing my dad of favoritism when he was calling his own son out on strikes. And you know what? They were strikes.

I played pitcher and first base when I was 6 to 7 years old. When I got drafted to play with the 12-year-olds, my dad wouldn't let me play because they were too much older than me.

—*Brady Anderson*

HITTING

PART 5

BUNTING FOR A BASE HIT OR SACRIFICE

LUIS ALICEA

Bunting isn't usually featured on the highlight shows every night. But while it may not pack the same punch as a home run, a well-executed bunt can prove to be a pivotal play in a team's rally. That goes for a sacrifice bunt as well as a bunt for a hit.

In this chapter, versatile switch-hitter Luis Alicea explains how to successfully drop down each type of bunt, from each side of the plate.

How do you drop down a sacrifice bunt?

There are two ways you can bunt to **give yourself up** and move the runner up a base. One way is pivoting. In this case, you **pivot** your body in the batter's box and put the bat in front of you.

What do you do with your hands?

The bottom hand doesn't move. The other hand should slide up to the label of the bat.

What position should the bat be in, besides in front of you?

The bat should stay at a 45-degree angle. The **barrel** of the bat has to remain above the ball. That way, when the ball hits the bat, the ball has to go down. You always want the bunt on the ground and not in the air. If the barrel is below your hands, the ball has a tendency to fly up when it's hit. And that's going to be a popup or a foul ball, which means you won't get the job done. Your hands can't be stiff. The bat has to be gripped softly so the ball doesn't jump off the bat.

Suppose the pitch is down in the strike zone?

If the pitch is low, bend your knees and try to keep the 45-degree angle. Don't just reach for the ball with the bat.

When you're bunting, the barrel of your bat acts like a glove. You're actually trying to simulate catching the ball with the barrel of the bat to soften the blow so you don't bunt too hard.

What's the other method to dropping down a sacrifice bunt?

Squaring around. In this instance, take your back foot and bring it around in the batter's box so you're actually facing the pitcher. Don't even think about getting a hit this way. You're sacrificing yourself to move the runner up a base.

128

Which sacrifice bunt approach is best, pivoting or squaring around?

When you square and face the pitcher, your back foot will be just a few inches from the plate, so you can actually cover more of the plate with your bat. That's why, when you sacrifice, some coaches want you to do it that way. If the pitcher makes a tough pitch, you'll still be able to get out there and bunt it. But both the pivoting and squaring approaches can be successful.

Is there any drawback in trying to bunt by squaring around?

It's a little dangerous, because if the ball comes right at you, you have less of a chance to get away from it. When facing pitchers who are somewhat wild, it is not a good idea to square to bunt. You might get hit.

Do you handle the bat any differently when using this method?

The technique with the bat stays the same. Your bottom hand stays where it is, while the other hand slides up the barrel to the bat's label. Keep that 45-degree angle with the bat too. The main thing is to get the ball down on the ground, either to third base or to first base.

When you slide your hand up to the label, do you wrap your fingers around the bat?

No. Grip the bat by folding your knuckles around it. You should let it rest between your index finger and your thumb. Then bend the knuckles of your other fingers behind the bat.

Why this kind of grip?

It helps you to soften the impact of the ball as it hits the bat. If you have a very firm grip, with your fingers tightly wrapped around the bat, the ball will hit harder and it may have a bigger bounce. Plus, you run the risk of having the ball hit your knuckles, causing an injury.

Why don't you want to hit the bunt with a big bounce?

You always want the fielders to come in to get the ball. You don't want the ball to come to them. That would just make it easier for them to make a play on the baserunner.

Is there any particular place you want to bunt the ball?

You don't want your bunt to pass the pitcher's mound. That would mean you bunted the ball too hard. Try to bunt directly to either the third baseman or the first baseman. But you always want to make the fielders come halfway from their position to the plate for the ball.

How do you bunt for a base hit?

As a right-handed hitter, you need to make a **jab step,** which is when your right foot moves back slightly as the pitch comes to the plate. This will position your body and start your momentum to first base.

But remember, timing is important. When you're bunting for a base hit, don't let the defense know it. Start your jab step just as the pitcher is about to throw the ball. If you do this too early, the fielders will break in for the bunt and get there faster to throw you out.

What do you do with the bat as you make the jab step?

Point your bat toward first base. That way, your bat will be at the proper angle to bunt toward third base, which is usually where you want to bunt as a right-handed hitter. Sometimes, though, a left-handed pitcher will fall off the mound toward third-base in his follow-through. If that happens, your better chance for a hit would be to push the ball past the mound toward the second baseman.

Where do you bunt the ball if you're a left-handed hitter?

If you're a left-handed hitter, you'll probably want to bunt down the third-base line. The key is placement. You need to place the ball 2 to 3 feet from the foul line. That makes it a very tough play for the third baseman. If he's playing away from the line, he has to come all the way back to it, get the ball, and then make an awkward throw. It's also a next-to-impossible play for the pitcher.

Do you use a jab step when bunting for a hit as a left-hander?

In that case, you would actually use the pivot move. Sometimes it looks as if a left-hander is running out of the box as he bunts. But you actually have to stay in the box and wait for the ball a little longer.

Why wouldn't you try to bunt the ball as you run out of the batter's box, in order to get a head start to first base?

Sometimes you'll miss the pitch. Or you might figure the pitch isn't over the plate, when it really is. You come out of the **hitting zone** when you run out of the batter's box too soon and you can't really tell what's a strike. Always stay in the hitting zone until the ball crosses the plate.

What's a good pitch to bunt for a hit?

You actually want to bunt a ball that's on the inner part of the plate. If the ball is away, you have a tendency to reach for it and you might accidentally pop it up. Always **zone in** on an area for the pitch. If the ball is in your area, go for the bunt. If it's not in that area, then lay off.

Where on the bat do you want to bunt the ball?

You want to bunt the ball on the last 6 to 8 inches of your bat. The closer to the end of the bat, the softer the ball will come off. If you

bunt the ball on the meat of the bat, the ball will shoot out and reach the fielders much faster.

As a left-handed hitter, how do you pull a bunt past the pitcher's mound?

That's called a drag bunt. You have to pivot. Point the bat at third base and raise the bat's angle. On this type of bunt, you actually do not want to hit the ball too softly. You want the ball to get past the pitcher's mound. You're aiming the ball directly at the second baseman. A drag bunt gives you a half-step running head start to first base.

GLOSSARY

Barrel: The fattest part, or "meat," of the bat. This is where you want to hit or bunt the ball.

Give yourself up: To willingly make an out in order to successfully move the runner (or runners) up a base.

Hitting zone: The area in which a ball arrives at home plate. It is generally the strike zone, where a pitch would be called a strike if the hitter let it go by.

Jab step: As a right-handed batter, a quick step back with the right foot as the pitch approaches the plate.

Pivot: To turn or twist your body.

Zone in: To look for a pitch in a certain area of the hitting zone when hitting or bunting.

THEN I'LL HUFF, AND I'LL PUFF . . .

It's possible for a player to become winded every now and then. But the Kansas City Royals' Kevin Seitzer took that expression literally in a June 9, 1987, game against Minnesota.

Seitzer was playing third base. Until the eighth inning, it was a typical game. The Twins were leading 4–2, with two runners on base. Dan Gladden stepped into the batter's box to face Royals' pitcher Steve Farr and decided to drop down a bunt. The ball went rolling slowly down the third-base line on the artificial turf in the Metrodome. Seitzer knew instantly he didn't have a play. Even if he charged the ball, he would have no chance to throw out Gladden. Plus, he couldn't make a play at any other base either.

In these situations, the fielder will often let the ball go, hoping it will roll into foul territory. But because they were playing on artificial turf, Seitzer knew the ball would roll on a straight path and it would stay fair.

There didn't seem to be much Seitzer could do about it. But the quick-thinking infielder made an attempt.

Seitzer dropped to his knees, got his body down low to the turf, took a deep breath, and tried to blow the ball into foul territory as it continued to roll. He crawled up the baseline with the ball, his face inches from the turf, huffing and puffing the whole way—determined to blow the ball into foul territory.

It was a nice try. But apparently Seitzer wasn't a big enough windbag, because the ball stayed fair. Gladden was credited with a base hit, and the Twins ultimately scored a run later in the inning, breezing to a 5–2 win.

HERE'S THE SITUATION

It's the last inning. Your team is losing by three runs and you're leading off. You look down the third-base line and notice that the third baseman is playing pretty deep. You're not a power hitter, though you have hit a few home runs in your career. You're very good at putting the bat on the ball and you run pretty fast.

Should you swing for the fences? Or should you try to bunt for a base hit?

HERE'S THE SOLUTION

Drop one down.

Take the chance on bunting for a base hit. Trailing by three runs, your team needs baserunners. You can't tie the game until you have two runners on base. So even if you hit a home run, your team still will be two runs down. Plus, you're more likely to make an out than hit a home run if you try to swing for the fences.

If you have speed and can make contact and the third baseman is playing deep, dropping a bunt down is a good plan. It will force the third baseman to make a tough play. And if your bunt is even halfway decent, you're likely to get on base to start a rally.

★★★★★ **MEMORIES** ★★★★★

I grew up in Guaynabo, Puerto Rico, which is a metropolitan area 10 minutes away from San Juan. Baseball was *the* sport to play. I'd play on two or three teams at a time, in organized leagues. That's all it was back then—baseball, baseball, baseball.

One of the most memorable teams I played on when I was 13 or 14 was called "Napa." "Napa" means "the leftovers"...like having a chip on your shoulder because you're the kids who weren't the first ones chosen. My dad built a team with guys like that. At first, I didn't want to play there because it was filled with players that nobody really wanted on their team. But we became a good team and even made it to the finals. We ended up losing to another team that was hand-picked for the finals. But it was a big accomplishment just to get there in the first place.

I pitched and played shortstop and outfield. I remember pitching one game and playing short the next. I was real scrappy. I didn't have a lot of power. I'd get on base a lot though. I was a leadoff hitter most of the time. At that age, I could run really fast. I was the smallest guy on the team but they called me pimienta, which is the pepper on the team. You never get tired when you're a kid.

We played on different types of fields. In my area, we were fortunate enough to have two good fields where many state tournaments were held. The majority of fields were decent. They had fences and were designed for Little League Baseball. We had lights, too.

When I was young, I played against future big leaguers such as Ruben Sierra, Benito Santiago, Sandy and Roberto Alomar, Carlos Baerga, Rey Sanchez, Orlando Merced, Edwin Correa, and Juan Nieves. We were all kids and just having fun.

A lot of times we played doubleheaders. After the first game, all the parents and families would get together. The parents would take turns bringing food. One week my parents would bring the sandwiches. The next week someone else would bring them. They used to give us a lot of soup and sandwiches. It was really great, a very family-like atmosphere.

BASIC HITTING FUNDAMENTALS

WADE BOGGS

Some people say that the most difficult task in all of sports is trying to hit a round ball squarely with a round bat. If the ball isn't hit squarely, it isn't likely to travel very far, nor will it be hit very hard. So it's important to keep your eye on the ball.

In this chapter, future Hall-of-Famer Wade Boggs offers a few suggestions on how to see and hit the ball.

What is your basic theory of hitting?

When you're starting out at a young age, I like to talk about the "Wait-Weight" theory.

What does that mean?

It means you *wait* on the ball as long as you can and then you transfer your body *weight* on a good swing. Too many kids want to rush out to the ball. They never wait on the ball to get to them. You also have to keep your head down when you're hitting. That's the only way to keep your eye on the ball.

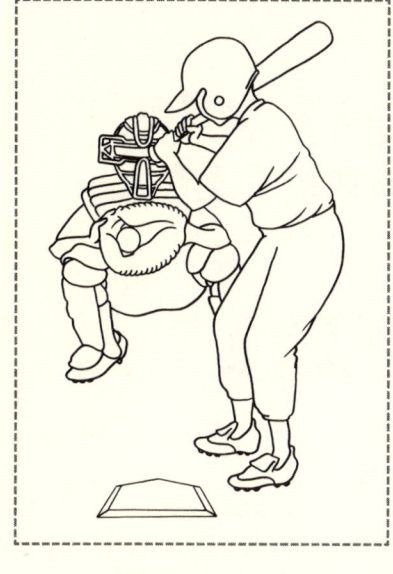

Why is it important to keep your eye on the ball?

Well you can't hit what you can't see! That's why you want to keep your head down on the baseball. If you pull your head off the ball, you're not going to make solid contact.

I used to watch every pitch right into the catcher's mitt when I didn't swing. I started doing that when I was 7 or 8 years old. It gives you a longer look when you're taking a pitch. You track it all the way, right to the catcher's mitt. It's good practice for making you **stay on the ball** longer and helping you wait longer.

How do you become a good hitter?

When you're young, the biggest thing is to practice. Get a parent or sibling out in the backyard and have them throw Wiffle balls to you. Or get other kids in the neighborhood to play Wiffle ball games. Get a broomstick and hit a tennis ball—anything that will help you practice!

Should kids try to hit home runs?

Small kids shouldn't try to hit home runs. That's not going to be their type of game. They should try and work on hitting **line drives.**

You accommodate your swing by your size. If you're a big kid at 12 years old, you can work on **driving the ball** and hitting home runs. But if you're a small second baseman, for instance, you have to find something you can do to help the team win. Hitting line drives could be your game.

When the pitch comes and you start your swing, do you jump out at the pitch?

No, it's more of a pendulum effect. Think of an old grandfather clock, where the pendulum swings back and forth. In order to generate more **bat speed** and power, you shift your weight back a bit before moving forward when the pitch comes. That's what's called the weight transfer.

You can also think of slamming a door. If the door is half open and you slam it shut from that position, the door will bang a little. But if you take that door and bring it back even farther before you push it forward, it will cause a much louder bang.

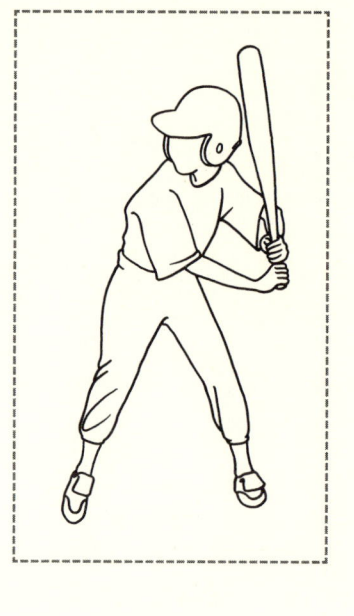

GLOSSARY

Bat speed: The speed of the bat generated by the swing.

Driving the ball: Hitting the ball hard and deep to the outfield.

Line drive: A ball that is hit in the air, but not as high as a fly ball. Line drives typically are hit hard.

Stay on the ball: Keeping your eye on the ball as long as possible, which gives you a better chance to hit the ball well.

★★★★★★★★★★★★★★★★★★★★★★★★★

THE EYES HAVE IT!

Wade Boggs had one of the best batting eyes in the history of the Major Leagues. Not only did he use his keen eyesight to notch 3,010 hits, but he also drew 1,412 walks in his 2,440-game career. No one watched the ball all the way into the catcher's mitt better than Boggs. He refused to swing unless he saw a pitch he thought he could hit well.

And in Game 4 of the 1996 World Series, Boggs's patience paid off.

The game was tied at 6–6, heading into the tenth inning. When Wade Boggs stepped to the plate, there were two outs and the bases were loaded with Yankees. Boggs fell behind in the count 1–2, then took some close pitches that were called balls. Finally, on a 3-and-2 pitch, Boggs took another close pitch, which was also called a ball. He had earned a walk, and the tie-breaking run was forced in. The Yankees went on to win the game—and eventually, the 1996 World Series!

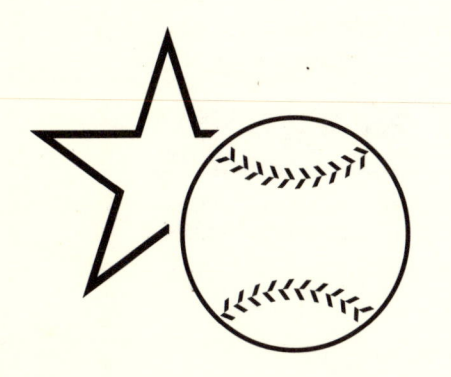

HERE'S THE SITUATION

The pitcher you're facing is a little wild. He has walked the last two batters and thrown just one strike out of his last nine pitches. There are runners at first and second, with no one out. It's the third inning and your team is behind by five runs. It's your turn to hit. You step in the batter's box and swing your bat back and forth, getting ready for the first pitch.

Should you swing at that first pitch, guessing that the pitcher is due to throw a strike?

★ ★ ★ ★ ★ ★ ★ ★ ★ ★ ★ ★ ★ ★ ★ ★ ★ ★

HERE'S THE SOLUTION

It might be a good idea to take the first pitch, even if it turns out to be a strike. Clearly, the pitcher is struggling. You're down by five runs, so the more runners you can get on base, the quicker you'll have an opportunity to catch up.

It's okay if that first pitch turns out to be a strike. The pressure is still on the pitcher. If he's wild, there are good odds that he's just trying to throw a strike and not worrying too much about how hard the ball is thrown. If you have confidence in yourself as a hitter, you'll be ready if the pitcher is able to throw his next pitch for a strike. Besides, taking a pitch every now and then can help you practice watching the ball all the way into the catcher's mitt.

If the first two pitches are out of the strike zone, you might want to consider taking more pitches until this pitcher proves he can throw a strike. Even a walk in this situation would be helpful to your team because it would load the bases and keep the rally going.

★ ★ ★ ★ ★ MEMORIES ★ ★ ★ ★ ★

The last Little League memory I have was an All-Star game I played in for the Bayshore Little League in Tampa, Florida. I was 2 for 2, the only kid in the game with two hits, and I got replaced by a pinch-hitter. I never figured that one out.

I played for the Elks team in Brunswick, Georgia, and for the Bayshore Buicks in Tampa. I didn't start hitting home runs until I was 13. I hit one in Little League. I remember that at-bat. It was off a left-handed pitcher. I had hit seven foul home runs and then the next one finally went straight down the left-field line for a fair home run.

I was just a small, scrawny kid in Little League, probably 5-feet tall when I was 12 years old, and maybe 100 pounds soaking wet!

Wade Boggs

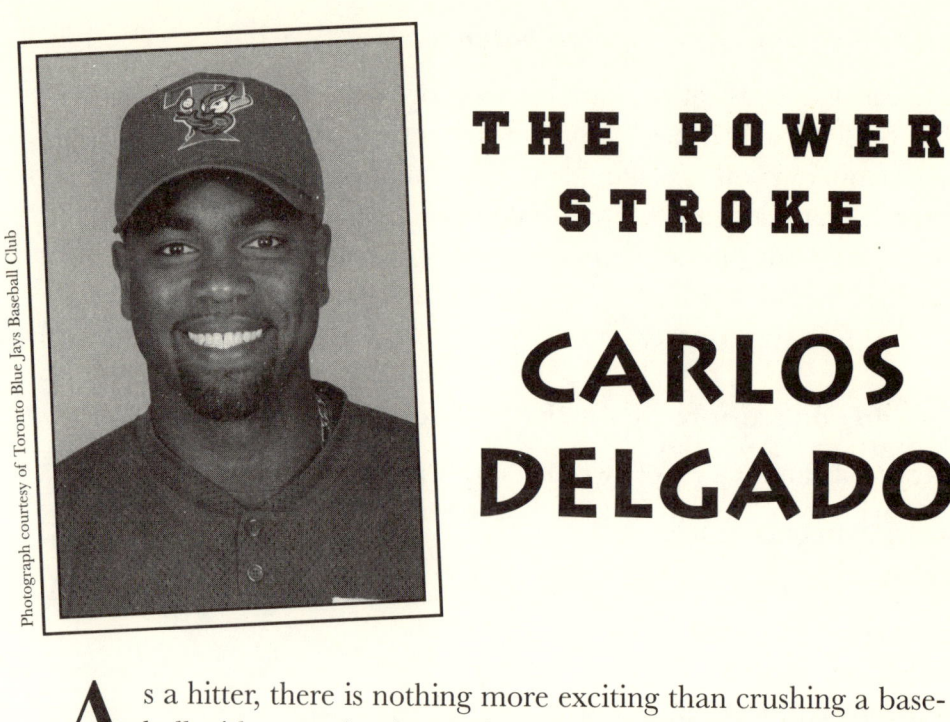

THE POWER STROKE

CARLOS DELGADO

As a hitter, there is nothing more exciting than crushing a baseball with a good swing and sending it flying over the fence. The home run trot that follows is about as good as it gets! Sheer strength can be helpful in hitting home runs. But it isn't just the biggest and strongest batters who hit the ball out of the park.

In this chapter, All-Star home run champion Carlos Delgado analyzes techniques to help a batter hit for power.

Is there one stance you should use?

I think everybody has his own preferred stance.

One thing about hitting is that you have to be comfortable and you have to stick with what works. I always say it doesn't matter what stance you use, but choose a stance where you have balance. You're going to be shifting and moving a lot during your swing, so at some point you have to generate some power through **torque.** When you turn your hips and really get into the swing, you'll have the right balance and the good foundation you need.

How do you stand so you're balanced?

Basically, you want to be on the balls of your feet. You don't want to be back on your heels. The distance between your feet shouldn't be too narrow, but you also shouldn't spread your feet out too much either. It's harder to move around that way. Your feet don't necessarily have to be shoulder-width apart, like some people might say. You have to adjust to what feels right to you. Just make sure you're balanced and that you find your comfort zone.

Why do you want to be on the balls of your feet?

So you can do a lot of twisting and shifting while you're taking your swing. You have to rock back when the ball starts coming toward you to create momentum. Then you have to go forward and attack the ball when it's time to swing. Being on the balls of your feet is very important when it comes to that.

What do you look at when you're at the plate?

You should always look at the pitcher. It sounds very simple, but sometimes batters forget. You have to be focused on the exact point where the pitcher will release the ball. Then you have to follow the ball with your eyes all the way toward home plate.

How much does your head move?

Your head should move as little as possible. If your head is moving, you won't see the ball as well as you need to.

During your swing, you want to move your legs and your torso. You also want your hands and bat to move back a little before they go forward to hit the ball. Always keep your head in the same spot. You start your swing and continue it with your head in the same spot, looking at the ball the whole time.

Why is that?

If you're 9 or 10 years old, you might just be seeing fastballs. But as you get older, the pitchers will put a little curve on the ball, or the ball may have late movement when it gets to the plate. So you want to recognize exactly what the ball is doing, and adjust to it. In order to do that, you have to watch the ball the whole way to the plate. And to see the ball best, you should keep your head as still as possible.

What other part of the body is important in hitting?

The front shoulder is very important. It should be pointed at the pitcher at all times. It's just like throwing. When you throw the ball, you point your front shoulder at your **target.** It's the same thing with hitting. Your shoulder and neck are attached to your head. If you move that front shoulder, your head will move, too.

So keep your front shoulder **closed.** That will keep your head in line with the pitcher. You'll be able to see—and hit—the ball better that way.

How important are your legs when hitting for power?

Your legs are your foundation. You need a lot of strength underneath you. But I think most of the power comes from your hands.

Why your hands?

You can have very strong legs but if your hands are slow, you're not going to generate much power. You have to be able to "explode" with your hands.

Which hand on the bat helps you most when you're trying to generate power?

Your bottom hand on the bat is very important in hitting for power. That's the hand that gets the bat going. The guys who are

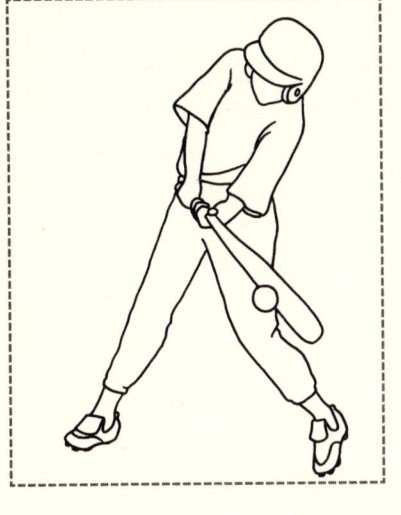

really strong, but don't hit the ball out of the park, usually do not generate enough **bat speed.** And it's the bottom hand on the bat that generates the bat speed through the hitting zone.

Hitting for power is not just about muscles. It's about bat speed. You see some small guys who have quick wrists and a quick bat, and they can hit for power. You can have all the movement you want with your legs, but if you don't get your hands going, you're not going to hit well. People have different theories on this, but I try to hit with my hands—not with my body, and not with my legs. That works for me.

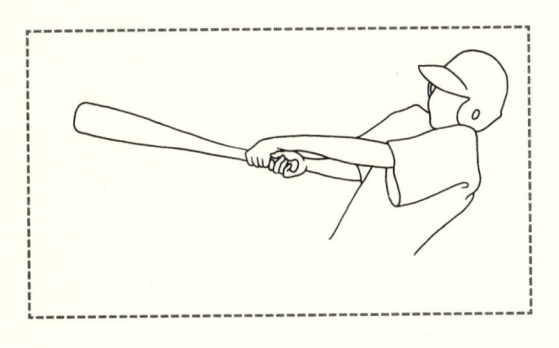

Describe the actual process of hitting the baseball.

I want to hit the ball as if I'm slapping it with the back of my bottom hand. I want my bottom hand to get to the ball as quickly as possible. And when I finish off my swing, I want to get good **extension.**

What does your top hand do?

It gives you extension!

I try to avoid having my top hand come through too hard. If it does, it will **roll over** my bottom hand. And since I'm a left-hander, that means I'll hit a lot of ground balls to second base. When your top hand rolls over, you get too much **topspin** on the ball, and the ball won't **carry.** You want **backspin.** Try to hit the ball slightly underneath. You won't be able to do that if your top hand comes through too hard.

146

How can you avoid rolling over?

That's where your bottom hand comes into play. If the bottom hand leads the bat through the zone, it's pretty hard to roll over. I'm naturally right-handed, but because I bat left-handed, my bottom (right) hand is my **dominant** hand. Leading with your bottom hand helps you have more control of the bat, as well as your power.

What kind of follow-through do you recommend to hit for power?

The kind of pitch the pitcher throws determines how you follow through on your swing. If the pitch is away on the outside of the plate, you should keep going that way with the bat. If the pitch is on the inside part of the plate, then you should try to keep your hands inside and finish straight ahead. Don't spin off.

Do you follow through with both hands on the bat or do you let the top hand come off?

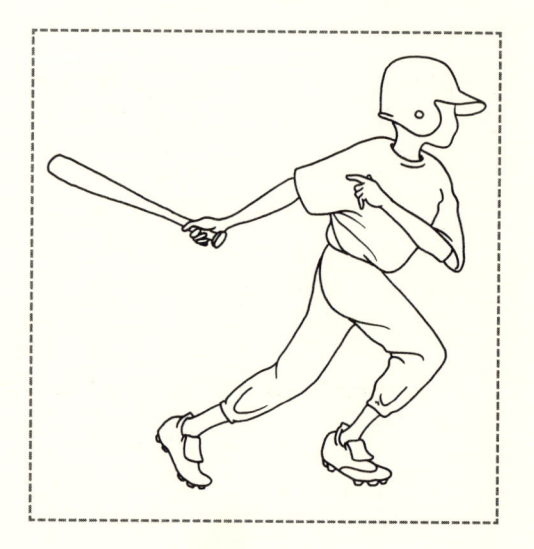

Eventually, your top hand naturally comes off. But you don't want it to release until after you've hit the ball. Sometimes you want to keep both hands on the bat when you follow through. Ideally, if you **stay back** and hit the ball well, your top hand should stay on the bat.

How often do you actually try to hit a home run?

The worst thing I can do is to try to hit home runs! I tend not to get very good bat speed that way and my swing isn't as quick. You want a short swing. Why? The longer the swing, the longer it takes to move the bat through the **hitting zone**—and the pitch may get past you.

So instead of trying for home runs, I just try to get hits. I always try to hit the ball hard. When I'm in a good groove, I aim to hit **line drives up the middle.** That way, if my timing's a bit off but I still hit the ball, I can get a base hit to left or right field.

Whenever I try to hit home runs, it never happens. So I just don't try anymore!

How can a young person practice generating bat speed?

There are a lot of ways to increase bat speed. You can do a **soft toss** drill, hit a ball off a tee, or take batting practice off a pitching machine. But you have to work at it. You have to do it over and over. Repetition is very important. Keep your bottom hand going through the swing. And keep your swing as short as you can.

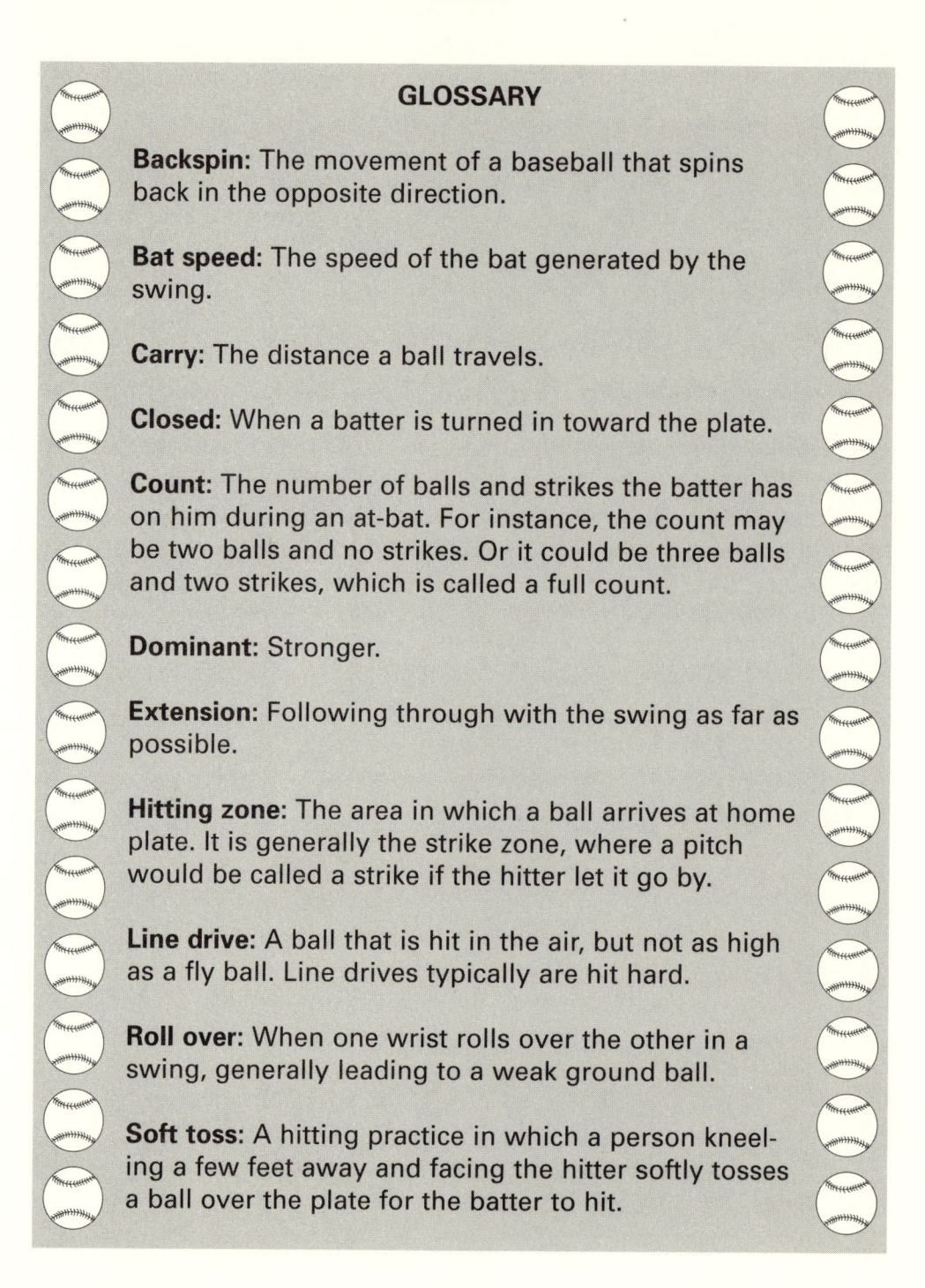

GLOSSARY

Backspin: The movement of a baseball that spins back in the opposite direction.

Bat speed: The speed of the bat generated by the swing.

Carry: The distance a ball travels.

Closed: When a batter is turned in toward the plate.

Count: The number of balls and strikes the batter has on him during an at-bat. For instance, the count may be two balls and no strikes. Or it could be three balls and two strikes, which is called a full count.

Dominant: Stronger.

Extension: Following through with the swing as far as possible.

Hitting zone: The area in which a ball arrives at home plate. It is generally the strike zone, where a pitch would be called a strike if the hitter let it go by.

Line drive: A ball that is hit in the air, but not as high as a fly ball. Line drives typically are hit hard.

Roll over: When one wrist rolls over the other in a swing, generally leading to a weak ground ball.

Soft toss: A hitting practice in which a person kneeling a few feet away and facing the hitter softly tosses a ball over the plate for the batter to hit.

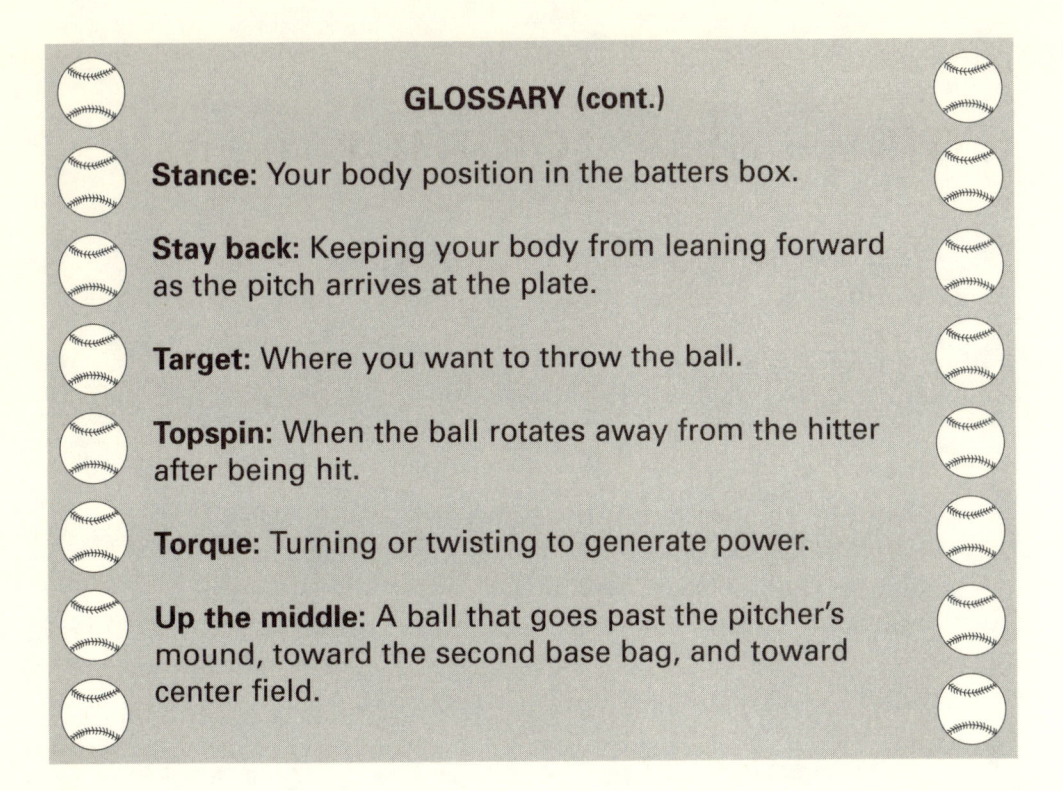

GLOSSARY (cont.)

Stance: Your body position in the batters box.

Stay back: Keeping your body from leaning forward as the pitch arrives at the plate.

Target: Where you want to throw the ball.

Topspin: When the ball rotates away from the hitter after being hit.

Torque: Turning or twisting to generate power.

Up the middle: A ball that goes past the pitcher's mound, toward the second base bag, and toward center field.

THREE CHEERS FOR THE POWERFUL LITTLE GUY!

It's not unheard of for a player to hit three home runs in a game. Generally, such power displays are reserved for the biggest sluggers in the majors. For example, power hitter Sammy Sosa blasted three homers in one game—not once, but twice—in August 2001. But maybe that's not so incredible, considering Sosa is a well muscled, 6-foot, 210-pounder.

However, Freddie Patek accomplished the same feat about 21 seasons ago. Patek was a small infielder, standing about 5-foot-5 and weighing a mere 148 pounds. He was better known for his defensive abilities in his 14 big-league seasons, rather than his home run hitting ability. In fact, in his 1,650 major league games, Patek hit just 41 home runs...or 25 fewer than Sosa hit in 1998 alone!

But on June 20, 1980, Patek launched three home runs out of Boston's Fenway Park, leading the California Angels to a 20–2 rout of the Red Sox. Patek, who also had a double in the game, hit solo, two-run, and three-run homers.

Patek only hit two other homers for the rest of the year. He finished the season with a total of five. And he never hit more than six home runs in any of his other major league seasons. But on that one night, Freddie Patek showed the baseball world that hitting home runs was not strictly for the big guys.

HERE'S THE SITUATION

There are two runners on base when you step into the batter's box. The game is tied up in the later innings. The **count** is 2 and 0. The next pitch is on the outside corner, about knee high. It's a borderline strike. Maybe it will be called a strike, but there's a chance that it could also be called a ball.

Should you swing?

HERE'S THE SOLUTION

Take the pitch.

When the count is 2–0, or even 3–1, those are called hitter's counts. This means that the hitter can be selective on which pitch he chooses to swing at. When a hitter is ahead in the count, there's no need to swing at a tough pitch…even if it's a strike. The odds of squarely hitting a tough pitch are not good, so there's no reason to help out the pitcher.

So take the tough pitch. Even if it's called a strike, the pitcher still has to throw a strike on his next pitch at 2–1 or 3–2. And it's not that easy for a pitcher to make two tough pitches in a row. The odds are in your favor that the next pitch will be a good one to hit.

Of course, taking a pitch requires discipline at the plate. If you see a pitch you think you can hit, you may immediately want to swing at it. But if you have confidence as a hitter, you also know you can wait for the better pitch.

★★★★★ **MEMORIES** ★★★★★

I played in the Little Leagues in Aguadilla, Puerto Rico. That's the town where I grew up. I didn't think about playing in the big leagues when I was 9. I just went out to play and have fun.

We played for different teams. Most of the time we played in one local league. The teams changed every year. But whenever the game was over, we'd get hot dogs and pizza. That was pretty cool.

We'd always play our games on Saturday mornings. I really looked forward to them. At 7:30 A.M., I'd be sitting on our living room couch, waiting for my mom to take me to the game. I'd have on my uniform and spikes. I'd be watching cartoons, just waiting for it to be game time.

There were times when I pitched, but mostly I was a catcher. If you won the league at the end of the season, you got to go play in different towns. That was a lot of fun. You'd go away for a week or a weekend, and stay in the local gymnasium. There'd be about 15 to 20 of your friends, all staying together. We just had a good time jumping around. It was great.

I wasn't a home run hitter when I was little. I didn't become a home run hitter until I was 16, a year before I signed a professional contract. Home runs are cool now, but you have to get the little hits first. Hitting home runs will come later.

Where I came from, we didn't play on perfect baseball fields. We didn't have the facilities they have in some places in the United States, but I didn't play on dirt fields with rocks all over the place, either. It was just a regular field, with grass on the infield. It was good enough. All our parents and friends came to the games. It was just great to be able to play.

THE ART OF CLUTCH HITTING

Photograph courtesy of Anaheim Angels/Lovero Group

MO VAUGHN

As a hitter, you feel pressure each time you step into the batter's box. There's no one to help you out—it's just you and the pitcher. But the pressure level rises when there are runners on base in a tight game and you're the one up at bat. Your teammates are counting on you to come through to help win the game. The butterflies are dancing in your stomach. It's not unusual for a batter to be nervous in this important situation.

In this chapter, MVP first baseman Mo Vaughn talks about how to conquer nerves—and turn that energy into a positive and productive at-bat.

When runners are in scoring position late in a close game, who do you think feels more pressure: the batter or the pitcher?

There's always pressure on the hitter when there are **runners in scoring position.**

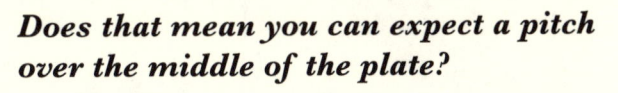

But the main thing you have to do is to mentally transfer that pressure from yourself to the pitcher. Realize that the pitcher is the one in the tough situation, because he has to make the tough pitch to try and get *you* out.

But no matter how much pressure you or the pitcher may feel, you always want to pick the right pitch to hit.

Does that mean you can expect a pitch over the middle of the plate?

The number of outs on the board when you step to the plate indicates how the pitcher is going to come after you. If there's one out and a man on second, that's a different situation than having no outs or two outs. With runners on base, what kind of pitch you get—and where it will go—usually depends on three things: the **count,** the type of pitcher you're facing, and the number of outs.

How much does your concentration change in a clutch situation?

My concentration always increases when I have a chance to drive in runs.

You try to focus as much as you can in every at-bat, but you become even more intense when you're hitting with runners in scoring position.

Do you swing for home runs in those situations?

No. I always focus on who the pitcher is and how he might try to pitch me. I'm a lefty, so if I'm facing a left-handed pitcher, I might expect fastballs on the inside part of the plate, or **changeups** away. If

I get one of those pitches, I'll try to hit the ball to left field, the opposite field. On the other hand, a right-handed pitcher might try to pitch me on the outside part of the plate. So I always have to be ready for what they're trying to throw at me.

Batters who drive in a lot of runs are usually the guys who use the whole field. They can hit the ball all over the place, to every part of the field.

How difficult is it to control your emotions when you're hitting in a key spot in the game?

It's easier as you get older, since you have more experience. Then you *want* to be hitting in those types of situations all the time. I have a lot of fun with them. If the pitcher makes a mistake, our team is going to wind up winning.

I was confident when I was younger, but I wasn't very relaxed. Now it's easier for me to relax in tight situations. It's very important to stay relaxed when the game is on the line.

How did you start feeling relaxed at the plate?

It started by going up to the plate time and time again, being put in those situations a lot, so I could get comfortable with pressure. I have always batted third, fourth, or fifth in the lineup. When you're in one of those spots, you'll find yourself in those situations a lot.

Did you feel a lot of pressure when you were younger?

In Little League, I rarely got pitched to in clutch situations. The other teams would pitch to me only if they had to. I was always one of the bigger kids and I hit a lot of grand slams and home runs. That was fun.

GLOSSARY

Barrel: The fattest part, or "meat," of the bat. This is where you want to hit the ball.

Changeup: A pitch that looks like a fastball but is slower.

Count: The number of balls and strikes the batter has on him during an at-bat. For instance, the count may be two balls and no strikes. Or it could be three balls and two strikes, which is called a full count.

Runners in scoring position: Any runner on either second or third base is considered to be in scoring position because he usually can score from either base, on any kind of a hit.

★★★★★★★★★★★★★★★★★★★★★★★★★★

ARMED AND DANGEROUS— OR A REAL CORKER?

Albert Belle already had a reputation as one of the most powerful hitters in the game when he stepped to the plate in the eleventh inning of Game 1 of the American League Divisional playoffs. The Boston Red Sox were leading, 4–3 on October 3, 1995, at Cleveland's Jacobs Field.

But the lead didn't last long. Belle crushed a home run to left field off Rick Aguilera, tying the game at 4–4 and setting off stadium fireworks. However, Red Sox manager Kevin Kennedy suspected that Belle, who had hit 50 homers that season, was using a corked bat. So Kennedy demanded that the home plate umpire take the bat for further examination. If the bat had been corked, Belle would have been fined and suspended.

A corked bat is a bat that has been hollowed out from the top of the **barrel** down toward the label. The missing wood is replaced with cork, which is lighter and helps a batter swing the bat faster, generating more power than usual. In the Major Leagues, it is illegal to use a corked bat.

Belle's bat was sent to the umpire's room. Belle was absolutely furious. From the Cleveland dugout, he pulled up the right sleeve of his jersey and flexed his large biceps at Kennedy. He pointed at it and yelled that with his strength, he didn't need any illegal help.

The game eventually continued and the Indians won, 5–4. Cleveland ultimately swept

★★★★★★★★★★★★★★★★★★★★★★★★★★★★★★★

the series in three games. Belle's bat was x-rayed, and found not to have been corked.

But a few years later, the full story came out.

Jason Grimsley, a pitcher for Cleveland in 1995, came clean 4 years later, when he was pitching for the New York Yankees. He said he knew that Belle's bat was corked, so he climbed through a heating duct in the roof of the stadium and found his way into the umpires' room. He then exchanged a non-corked bat for the corked one without anyone seeing him. That's why the x-rays showed nothing but a regular bat.

Unfortunately for the Red Sox, Grimsley's confession came 4 years too late.

HERE'S THE SITUATION

The bases are loaded, there are two outs, and your team is two runs behind in the final inning. All kinds of questions are running through your mind.

Should you swing for the fences? Try to hit a grand slam? Should you swing as hard as you can? Should you swing if the ball is close to the plate, even if it's not a strike?

HERE'S THE SOLUTION

Relax.

Although it may be easier said than done, you should treat this at-bat as you would any other. You only want to swing at strikes. If the pitcher doesn't throw strikes, he'll walk you and force in a run. But you must always be ready for a strike. And if he throws one, take your normal swing. That's the best you can do. Wait for a good pitch and then try to hit it squarely with your best swing.

★★★★★ **MEMORIES** ★★★★★

From the age of 8 to 14, I played in the championship game every year, but my teams rarely won. When I was 12, I played for Magner's Funeral Home. We played in what they called the Cranberry Kinlock Tournament across the city in Norwalk, Connecticut. We weren't associated with the Little League, but we had a great system...and we used to beat up on the Little League teams. We were 18–0 during the regular season, but we lost in the championships. The year before that, we came in fourth place in the regular season, but won the championship.

I remember one year we played at a field that actually had dugouts and stands. There was a Little League field and then a softball field beyond it. I was hitting balls over the big fence of the softball field. I remember going 5 for 5 one day, with a couple of home runs and 7 RBI. That was a lot of fun!

—Mo Vaughn

PART 6

ON THE BASES

Photograph courtesy of Boston Red Sox

RUNDOWNS

JOHN VALENTIN

The runner is trapped between bases. His chances for survival are slim. But he doesn't give up. He keeps running back and forth between the bases, trying to avoid being tagged. He's in a situation commonly referred to as "being in a **pickle.**"

In this chapter, veteran infielder John Valentin discusses how to make sure the runner doesn't make it safely out of the pickle.

Let's say you're the second baseman and a runner is trapped between second base and third base. What do you do?

When you receive the ball as an infielder, the object is to be aggressive and force the baserunner to make a decision. If you have the baseball, run hard at him. He'll have no choice but to go in a certain direction. You don't want him floating back and forth between the bases.

165

You should run the guy down to a base and then throw the ball, so the baserunner doesn't have enough time to change direction. That's the easiest way to tag him out.

Where is the ball when you're trying to tag out a baserunner in a rundown?

If you're chasing a runner, hold the ball in your bare hand instead of your glove.

Why?

Because if the ball is in your glove, you have to go through the process of taking the ball out of the glove to make a throw. That takes more time, and you don't want to give the runner any extra time. Also, there's a chance you could mishandle the ball when taking it out of your glove.

Aren't there times when you'd want to have the ball in your glove?

It depends on how close the runner is to you. If the runner is running hard toward you, then you want to tag him with the ball in your glove because you're less likely to drop it if the runner bumps into you. But if you're going to make a throw in a rundown, you want the ball in your bare hand.

When you're chasing the runner and you have the ball in your throwing hand, do you fake throws?

No, you don't want to be faking throws. That makes it difficult for the guy who's going to catch your throw. He won't know if the ball is coming or not, and you don't want to fake him out. You just want to chase the runner with the ball in your hand and your arm up, ready to make a throw if the runner should commit to running to the base.

What kind of throw do you make in that situation?

It's a crisp, short, dart-like throw. That way, the person receiving the ball can see the throw coming, catch it easily, and then tag the runner.

How long do you hang onto the ball?

That depends on when you get it.

Let's say you're the second baseman and you pick a runner off second. You receive the throw from the pitcher or the catcher, and the rundown begins. If the runner is closer to the base in front of you, then you have to receive the ball and quickly throw it to the player at that base. He can then tag the runner if he's close enough, or he can run him hard in the opposite direction.

Do you always want to run the runner back to the base from where he came?

It's great if you have that luxury. At the very worst, he's back at the bag he started from even if you don't tag him out. But the object is to always get the out, no matter at which base.

If the runner is trapped off second base, and the second baseman has the ball, where does the third baseman position himself? Does he stand in the middle of the baseline?

It depends on where the second baseman receives the ball. You want to be on the same side of the **baseline** as the player who will make the throw. This will help you have a better view of the other defensive player and the ball you're about to catch. Also, the runner will have less opportunity to block your view, or get in the way of the throw.

In that situation, should the third baseman stand at the bag, waiting for the throw? Or should he move up a bit to shorten the rundown?

If you're about to catch the ball and there's a lot of space between you and your teammate, you definitely want to shorten the throw. So move up a little. Then you can tag out the runner immediately when the throw arrives.

Suppose you don't close up the rundown?

If you don't close it up, the runner can change direction and go back and forth. That means you'll be forced to make at least one other throw. And the more throws you make, the more risk there is you'll make a mistake. You should really try to get the runner out with only one or two throws.

GLOSSARY

Baseline: The path between the bases.

Pickle: A rundown.

Pivot: To turn or twist your body.

Short hop: A bounce that happens close to the fielder. It is just enough out of reach so that he can't catch the ball with his glove before it hits the ground.

Up the middle: A ball that goes past the pitcher's mound, toward the second base bag, and toward center field.

THE SACRIFICE THIGH

During the 1978 World Series, the New York Yankees' Reggie Jackson was involved in a controversial play.

Jackson was on first base when a soft, low liner was hit **up the middle.** The Los Angeles Dodgers' shortstop, Bill Russell, came racing in to make the play. Jackson wasn't sure if Russell would catch the ball in the air, or if it would hit the ground first. This caused Jackson some baserunning indecision. He started off first, then went back.

Russell, meanwhile, trapped the ball on one **short hop.** He didn't catch it in the air. He stepped on second base for a forceout. But when he threw to first for the double play, Jackson was in the baseline and the throw hit him on the thigh. The batter was safe at first. The Dodgers argued that Jackson had stuck his thigh out on purpose and therefore should have been called for interference. But the umpire didn't see it that way. No interference was called and the batter was safe at first.

Unfortunately for the Dodgers, that call wasn't the only thing to go New York's way. The Yankees won the Series, 4 games to 2.

HERE'S THE SITUATION

Runners are at first and third and there are two outs. Your team is ahead by a run, and it's the last inning. You're playing shortstop. The runner from first base takes off for second, trying to steal the bag. You cover second and take a good throw from the catcher. But the runner doesn't continue all the way to second. He gets in a rundown, trying to create enough confusion so the runner from third can sneak home and tie the game.

What do you do?

HERE'S THE SOLUTION

Start chasing the runner back to first base. At the same time, peek over toward third base to see what the runner there is doing. If the third-base runner breaks for the plate, quickly **pivot** and throw home. If he scores, the game will tied, so you want to make sure he doesn't score. But if he doesn't break toward home, continue to chase the first-base runner until you can apply the tag or throw the ball to the first baseman so he can do so.

★★★★★ MEMORIES ★★★★★

I grew up in the metropolitan area of New York City, on the New Jersey side. I was raised in Jersey City, where I went to Catholic schools. I played CYO, as well as Little League Baseball.

My memories are very good ones. Not to talk highly of myself, but I was a very good player back then in the Downtown Little League. I used to pitch and play shortstop. We had a good team. As a Little League pitcher, I had a good curveball but everyone told me my place was at short-stop.

The name of my team was Pepsi-Cola, because they pretty much sponsored the whole league. So after the game, we would all drink Pepsi.

I took a lot of pride in my defense, even defense as a pitcher. I was quick off the mound on any bunts and I made the plays. I didn't know my future was going to be in base-ball but it was exciting to be in an organized league.

I was a classic number two hitter. I used to bunt a lot and do hit-and-runs, too. I'd try to go the other way with the ball. But I was a pull hitter, so I usually hit the ball to the left side of the field most of the time. My uniform number was 3.

I didn't hit a home run until I went to high school. It was my senior year and I only hit one.

★ ★

RUNNING THE BASES

DARREN LEWIS

How hard can running the bases be? You hit the pitch and race to first base as fast as you can. Then it's on to second base, third base, and then home plate. But it's a lot more complicated than it seems. Baserunning is not just about speed, though being able to run fast is a big plus. There's much more to it than just that.

In this chapter, Darren Lewis, one of the game's best baserunners, offers some helpful hints for use on the base paths.

What's the first thing you do after you hit the ball?

The main thing is to get out of the batter's box quickly. After you do, run hard and run straight up the line because the shortest distance between two points is a straight line. And always run straight through the bag. You never want to run to the bag and just stop.

Why not just stop at the bag?

If you run through the bag, you're actually accelerating as you get there. If you are running just to get to the bag, you're going to slow down as you reach it. It's almost as if you want to keep running through to the outfield. You'll have a better chance of being safe this way.

What do you do when you hit the ball to left field and you know it's going to fall safely for a hit?

You run down the line and take the "banana route." You don't want to go too far into foul territory, but you want to give yourself an angle. That way, when you come through first base, you have as straight a line as possible to second base. It's not going to be like cutting on a football field. It's more like a curve around first base toward second base. That's where the term "banana route" comes in—the route is curved like a banana.

Do you watch the ball?

It depends on where the ball is hit.

If the ball is hit in the **gap,** for example right-center field, you can watch it while you're running. But let's say you hit a ground ball to the third baseman. Then you just put your head down and try to beat the throw to first. Once you run through the bag, then you **pick up the ball.** If it's a badly thrown ball past the first baseman, you'll be able to decide if you should try for second.

Why don't you want to be looking at a ground ball to third base, for instance?

You want to use all of your momentum on your straight line to first. If you're three-quarters of the way down the line and you look back, you're going to slow yourself down.

How do you round a bag to head to the next base? Which foot should hit the inside corner of the bag?

I was always taught that it depends on your comfort level. If you feel you get a better angle hitting the bag with your left foot, then that's what you should do. But if you think your right foot will work better, then go with your right. Again, it depends on your comfort level and your stride.

How do you slide on your legs?

Obviously it doesn't matter which knee you slide on, right or left. But you have to bend one under you. Just do what's comfortable.

One thing I learned at a young age was to stay away from the pop-up slide if you can. That's what players call a sit-down slide because you're almost sitting down on your slide. Then, as soon as you hit the bag, you pop back up onto your feet. Sometimes that slide can be deceptive to an umpire, making the play look closer than it really is. You might look as if you're out because you're coming up as the tag is being put down. But if you stay down on your slide, it may help give the umpire a different impression.

When you're running from first base and the batter gets a hit, when do you look at your third-base coach to tell you what to do?

One time you need to look up at your third-base coach is when you take off for second on a **hit-and-run.** Because you're running, you might not see the contact of the ball with the bat, so you can't be sure where the ball is headed. The other case is when you hit a triple. You let the third-base coach help you decide if you should try for third. Once you have more experience running the bases, you'll get a feel for where the ball is, what your speed is, and how many bases you can get.

But let's say you're on first base and there's a ball hit to right field. You know it's a hit. Do you look behind you for the ball or do you look to the third-base coach to give you direction?

As a 9- to 12-year-old, you'll probably check with your third-base coach. Glance toward him real quick and he'll either **hold you up** or wave you over to third.

Do you slow down as you're running when you glance over at the coach?

You should always run hard. You can run in that angle and pick up the third-base coach without losing any speed. Check with the third-base coach sometime before you hit second. If he holds you up, stop. If he gives you the signal to keep going, then keep on running. But the key is to not slow down.

Let's say you get caught in a rundown between second and third on a base hit. What do you do?

Stay in the **pickle** as long as you can. That will give the man from first base a chance to get to second. Even if you get tagged out, he'll be in **scoring position.** But hopefully the defense will make a mistake and you'll get out of the pickle.

GLOSSARY

Gap: The space between the outfielders, called left-center and right-center respectively.

Hit-and-run: An offensive play where the runner on first base runs for second as the pitch is thrown. The batter's responsibility is to swing and hit the ball on the ground, hopefully through an open part of the infield.

Hold you up: A signal from your third-base coach to stop.

Pick up the ball: To find the ball.

Pickle: A rundown.

Scoring position: Any runner on second or third base.

TWO FOR THE PRICE OF ONE!

Carlton Fisk was a very good catcher for the Boston Red Sox and the Chicago White Sox. He was so good in his 24 years in the big leagues that he was inducted into the Hall of Fame in Cooperstown, New York, in 2000. But in all of the games he caught in his long career, one of his most bizarre plays came on August 2, 1985, at Yankee Stadium.

It all began harmlessly enough in the bottom of the seventh, with the score tied at 3–3. Bobby Meacham was on second and Dale Berra was on first, for the Yankees. Rickey Henderson hit a long drive to left-center field. The Chicago center fielder, Luis Salazar, gave chase. Meacham held up, thinking the ball would be caught. But not Berra…he was running hard from the start. When the ball fell safely, Meacham finally began to run hard. Berra was right on his tail. Third-base coach Gene Michael waved Meacham home, and gave Berra the "stop sign" to stay put at third. But Berra was motoring around the base too fast to stop.

When the ball was relayed home to the plate, Fisk slapped a tag on Meacham. And then, reacting quickly, he dove and tagged out Berra too. Instead of a possible rally, New York did not score. The Yankees ultimately lost the game, 6–5!

HERE'S THE SITUATION

Your team is trailing by four runs and it's the last inning. You're leading off, and you hit a ball into the gap in right-center. The ball falls safely for a hit. As you round first base, you think you might have a chance to make it to second.

Should you try for a double?

HERE'S THE SOLUTION

It's always good to be aggressive on the base paths. But you also have to be smart.

If you are going to try for a double, you should be 100 percent certain that you can make it safely. At that point in the game, your run doesn't mean as much compared to the risk you're taking by trying for the extra base. You always want to get into scoring position. But the gamble to make it safely to second is probably not worth it because your team is down four runs. Take the single and hope your hit starts a big rally.

Now, if you were one run down in the same situation, you might want to take a chance and try for the double. If you make it safely, your team will have the tying run in scoring position with no one out.

★ ★ ★ ★ ★ MEMORIES ★ ★ ★ ★ ★

I grew up in Union City, California, which is a suburb of Oakland. I played in Union City National Little League from the time I was 8 to 18 years old. I have a lot of very good memories. It was a great program.

One specific memory was when we were about two games from the Senior Little League World Series. I was 14 years old. We went to the Western Regional and if we had won a couple more games, we would have gone to the World Series.

We played for Pete's Memorial. That was our team name because our coach's brother was killed in Vietnam. He had coached Little League for a very long time. Our coach's name was Bass Mendoza. Bass was one of the best Little League coaches you could ever have. He knew all the fundamentals. He really studied the game. He always had good teams. Everyone always wanted to play for his teams, too. It was a great experience for me.

We had white uniforms with black pinstripes, and red and black lettering on our uniforms. We wore black shoes with red stirrups and black hats. And our hats said "Pete's" on them. I was always number 11 in Little League. That was my favorite number. I played shortstop. From ages 9 to 12, I also played a bit of outfield, shortstop, third base, and second base. I actually pitched a little, too. It was a great program then, and it's still a great program now.

THE FINAL PITCH

By now you're probably ready to race back out to the diamond, fueled by all the information you've learned from this book. But remember, you won't become a Derek Jeter or a Pedro Martinez overnight! They weren't the big league stars they are now when they were your age, either.

Whether you're hitting the field for practice or playing a game, keep in mind the tips these twenty pros have offered. Their advice will help you to improve your skills and become the best baseball player you can be.

And as you pick up your glove and bat and head out to the field, remember one other very important thing.

Baseball is just a game.

Yes, you always want to play hard in a game. And you play to help your team win.

But here's the tip on which every big league player seems to agree, whether he's a pitcher, catcher, infielder, outfielder, or hitter.

Enjoy the game!

That's something the late Hall of Famer Willie Stargell did throughout his superb career with the Pittsburgh Pirates. "Pops," as he was called, never forgot the first baseball lesson he ever learned.

"Baseball's supposed to be fun," Stargell often said. "The (umpire) says 'Play ball,' not 'Work ball,' you know."

So get out to the field and have fun!

★ ★

ABOUT THE AUTHOR

STEVEN KRASNER has been a sports writer for *The Providence Journal* for more than twenty-five years, covering baseball as a beat writer for the Boston Red Sox since 1986. He is a graduate of Columbia University, where he played baseball and was team captain and MVP his senior year; he still plays in an adult men's league. Krasner has written four previous books for children, including *Why Not Call It Cow Juice?*, *The Longest Game*, *Have a Nice Nap, Humphrey*, and *Pedro Martinez*. He conducts an interactive writing program called "Nudging the Imagination" in schools and at conferences across the country. He lives with his family in Rhode Island.

★★★★★★★★★★★★★★★★★★★★★★★★★★

ACKNOWLEDGMENTS

The author would like to express his thanks and appreciation to the following people for their help in preparing this book:

Bill Almon; Bill Arnold; John Blake, Texas Rangers; Fred Bowen; Dick Bresciani, Boston Red Sox; Rob Butcher, Cincinnati Reds; Chris Costello, Tampa Bay Devil Rays; Megan Dimond, Philadelphia Phillies; Bill Gates, National Baseball Hall of Fame & Museum; Monique Giroux, Montreal Expos; Sean Harlin, Minnesota Twins; Diane Hock; Peggy Jackson; Emily Krasner; Tim Kurkjian, Tim Mead, Anaheim Angels; Paul Rappoli, Hit Dog Training Center; Gerard and Jeff Ratigan; Scott Reifort, Chicago White Sox; Matt Roebuck, Seattle Mariners; Kevin Shea, Boston Red Sox; Jay Stenhouse, Toronto Blue Jays; Bill Stetka, Baltimore Orioles; Bart Swain, Cleveland Indians; Leigh Tobin, Philadelphia Phillies; David Witty, Kansas City Royals; Jason Zillo, New York Yankees.